B E F O R E   t h e   A M E N

Before the Amen

Creative Resources for Worship

Maren C. Tirabassi and
Maria I. Tirabassi,
editors

THE PILGRIM PRESS
CLEVELAND

The Pilgrim Press, 700 Prospect Avenue, Cleveland, Ohio 44115
thepilgrimpress.com
2007 © Maren C. Tirabassi and Maria I. Tirabassi

Scripture quotations, unless otherwise noted, are from the New Revised Standard
Version of the Bible, © 1989 by the Division of Christian Education of the
National Council of Churches of Christ in the United States of America and
are used by permission. Changes have been made for inclusivity.

❀ Printed in the United States of America on acid-free paper that contains post-
consumer fiber.

15   14   13   12   8   7   6   5

Library of Congress Cataloging-in-Publication Data

Before the amen : creative resources for worship / Maren C. Tirabassi and
    Maria I. Tirabassi, eds.
        p. cm.
        Includes indexes.
        ISBN 978-0-8298-1750-8 (alk. paper)
        1. Worship programs.   I. Tirabassi, Maren C.   II. Tirabassi, Maria I., 1983–

BV198.B39 2007
264—dc22   2007043080

CONTENTS

PREFACE

"Amen" is derived from a Hebrew verb that means things like this: to take care, to support, to be firm or reliable, to trust in, to believe in. Jesus of Nazareth alone uses it to *introduce* his words of teaching; in the Synoptic gospels, we find "Amen, I say to you . . ." and in John, even more emphatically, "Amen, *amen*, I say to you. . . ." Throughout the rest of scripture "amen" comes afterwards as an affirmation or confirmation of what has gone before—often promise or praise. "Amen" can be solemn ratification and "amen" can be the burst-out assent to truth preached or prayed or presented or made person.

In our contemporary personal practice and congregational liturgy, "amen" is sometimes little more than nondescript punctuation. Too bad! Amen!

This is a book full of things that come before "amen," and we editors heard ourselves whispering, shouting, or singing "Amen!" over and over again as we received the liturgical gifts of eighty-four contributors to *Before the Amen*. We were moved, amazed and energized by prayers, litanies, services, songs, and dramatic pieces.

What follow are nine chapters of seasonal materials, three chapters of sacraments and services, and seven chapters oriented by topic. The boundaries are fuzzy—a generous browsing will locate, for example, elegant invitations to communion collected rather than dispersed into different seasons. A Lenten theme may appear under the chapters for "justice concerns" or "healing issues," and Labor Day materials are found under "civic concerns" rather than "ordinary time."

A startling discovery, since the publication of *Touch Holiness* seventeen years ago, is the diminished use of the *Revised Common Lectionary*. New lectionaries, local adaptations, and creative combinations are enriching worship life. To accommodate this shift and serve churches using the lectionary, we organized broad seasonal divisions within which liturgical offerings are arranged by beauty, poetry, and use of scripture, rather than divided by weeks. We cite scripture by chapter and verse in the text, but the scripture index simplifies the search by using only chapters. The topical index is designed to guide the reader to needed or unexpected gifts—such as blessing a Habitat house foundation or a church picnic, praying to enter a labyrinth, lamenting a dying church, or calling to worship for a "fair trade" service.

Before the Amen has three goals. The first is to serve as a straightforward reference to assist pastors or lay worship planners with bulletin materials. The second is to introduce worshiping congregations to incredible new liturgical voices. The third, and perhaps the most important, is as pump-primer—to inspire the reader to create new liturgies and shape new prayers about concerns we do not yet know, emboldened by the spirit found in these resources!

In other words—prayers. More prayers. Shared. *Amen!*

We appreciate the authors whose images became headings for the seasonal chapters—Molly Phinney Baskette, Susan E. Brown, Kathryn J. Campbell, Patricia Catellier, Abigail Hastings, Jamie Norwich McLennan, Nancy Rockwell, David Slater and Penelope J. Stokes. We were touched that Patricia Robbennolt offered her husband Roger's work and are honored to publish him posthumously. We are more than grateful to those in our home lives who have been patient with the time-intensive nature of anthology. For support, trust in us, and her own genius, thank you to Kim Martin Sadler. She is the kind of editor who makes an author's life a joy and shares not only skills but her own deep faith. Finally, for generosity and creativity beyond anything called duty, we thank Kristin Firth and Rick Porter for faithful care of the details of copy editing and layout!

—*Maren C. Tirabassi and Maria I. Tirabassi*

1

BEAUTIFUL TOES

Words for Advent

THE ONE WHO TESTIFIES
TO THESE THINGS SAYS,
"SURELY I AM COMING SOON."
AMEN. COME LORD JESUS!

Revelation 22:20

Tender Christ, in this sacred meantime, guard our hearts and prepare our minds, so that we may wait creatively, not distracted by the obligations of the season, nor unreadied by sloth. Prepare us, that at your coming we may recognize you and rejoice in your appearing. Grant us the courage to pray as people who believe in your appearing.

David Slater

Opening Prayer

In this blessed season, God, we must be thankful. First for the joy—the joy we hear raised in song, shared in a choir most triumphant, praising the story of Jesus' birth. Second, for the peace of these most quiet days, when the world remains still, as it was for the shepherds on lost hills. Third, God, for the love you have given us, for the love you showed when you told Mary that she need not be afraid, even in the midst of a most terrifying thing. And lastly, for Christ himself. Thank you for sending him to us to spread a message of forgiveness and acceptance to all people. We praise your name. Amen.

Maria I. Tirabassi

Call to Worship

We come together in these dark days.

We must look to you now to light our mornings and our evenings.

We come seeking renewed joy.

We must look now to each other for our spirits to be improved.

We come carrying gifts along with the burdens of the year.

We now look within to bring tidings of great joy.

Maria I. Tirabassi

Advent Poem · Luke 2:8–20

How hard it is to be patient, Child.
Your coming we anticipate.
Patience is not our strong suit, Child.
It is truly hard to wait.

We prepare gifts and food and cards
In many stops and starts.
But so often we forget, Child,
We first must prepare our hearts.

Shepherds saw your star, Child,
And were witnesses to your birth.
We await you as our shepherd,
God's caring love for earth.

Angels proclaimed your coming.
The good news was sung with joy.
We sing in joyous anticipation
Of the birth of this holy boy.

You have come among us, Holy Child,
Now a babe in a manger born.
But you will give your life for us,
Rising triumphant on Easter morn.

Mary Taylor

Call to Worship   ·   Isaiah 40:1–11

When we are lost, when we wander
off the path into the desert—

Gently, we are led by God.

When we crawl forward,
dragging our bodies across the sand,
tired and alone and thirsty—

Gently, we are led by God.

When all our good intentions lead us astray,
when they leave us with a dry, dusty tongue
that can no longer sing out the words of God—

Gently, we are led.

Maria I. Tirabassi

Opening Prayer for the Season of Advent

Merciful God, you sent your messengers the prophets
to preach repentance and to prepare the way of our salvation.
Give us grace to heed their words,
and to forsake our broken ways
that we may truly celebrate the remembrance of Jesus' birth.
We await with joy the coming glory of Christ our redeemer
who lives and reigns with you and the Holy Spirit,
one God forever and ever. Amen.

Jamie Norwich McLennan

Confession

God, we are not all as brave as Mary was. Often we hear your words and we are too afraid to take the gifts you have offered us. They seem too big and we would have to give up so much in order to receive them. We cannot see beyond our own trepidation, we cannot understand how anyone would want to follow such an uncertain path. We seek your blessings, God, but we also seek your understanding if we do not always understand them. There is a balance and we hope to hold it. Amen.

Assurance of Grace

Life is a balancing act between faith and fear. Choosing fear may not bring us the blessings we desire, but it also does not condemn us in the eyes of God. Thanks be for this forgiveness.

Maria I. Tirabassi

PREPARING THE CHRISTMAS TREE

First Week

This is the day bare branches are before us. We will take some time to help shape and mold these branches, for they've been packed away for many months. We do this to prepare the tree to receive Lights, Chrismons.

We are reminded by our shaping of these branches to shape ourselves: straighten up, be ready, look ahead, for God is going to do something wonderful in the very middle of our hearts and lives.

Let us pray:
Holy God, may the branches of this tree remind us of your arms that surround us. Amen.

We sing together:
O Christmas tree, O Christmas tree, you reach out to enfold us!
O Christmas tree, O Christmas tree, you reach out to enfold us!
Your branches offer us embrace, a sign of peace within this place.
O Christmas tree, O Christmas tree, you reach out to enfold us!

Second Week

There is a story that says on the first Christmas, to celebrate the holy birth, the stars came down out of the skies and rested on the branches of a fir tree. Some of the first Christmas trees were lighted with actual candles—only on Christmas Eve, and only with people to watch carefully!

This is the day we string some lights on our Christmas tree. Lights can be different colors and blink; they can be large or very small. Our lights are clear and bright! We place them on the tree's branches to brighten the inside of our church. They become visible reminders that *we* must shine out with love and caring, as God has done in Jesus Christ.

Let us pray:
Holy God, may the light on our tree remind us to be bright with your love.
Amen.

We sing together:
O Christmas tree, O Christmas tree, you tell of the Divine!
O Christmas tree, O Christmas tree, you tell of the Divine!
Revealing in sim-pli-city, Creator's touch of majesty,
O Christmas tree, O Christmas tree, you tell of the Divine!

Third Week

This week we place Chrismons on our tree. "Chrismon" is a word that combines the words "Christ" and "monogram." Chrismons traditionally are made of bright colors: white, clear crystal, silver, or gold—all to reflect light and to show the wonder of God's holy presence in Jesus Christ.

These symbols that speak to us of Christ tell a story of a life of selfless sharing and risking to spread the message of hope. God wants us to tell the good news with all our words and actions.

Let us pray:
Holy God, may these symbols remind us how close you are in Christ. Amen.

We sing together:
O Christmas tree, O Christmas tree, help us to share our story!
O Christmas tree, O Christmas tree, help us to share our story!
The Christ is born, Emmanuel: God in our midst—good news to tell!
O Christmas tree, O Christmas tree, help us to share our story!

Fourth Week

This week we place the star on the top of our tree. Sometimes an angel is placed at the top, for an angel appeared to Jesus' mother, Mary, many months before Jesus was born. And angels also sang the song of glory to God on the hillside of Bethlehem.

Whether a star, an angel, or even a Chrismon finds its way to the top of our tree, we are reminded to reach up and out, just like a tree, to be a living witness of good news we learn from Jesus, God's holy child.

Let us pray:
Holy God, may the top of our tree remind us that you are to be first in our hearts and lives. Amen.

We sing together:
O Christmas tree, O Christmas tree, you point the way to glory!
O Christmas tree, O Christmas tree, you point the way to glory!
With branches tall, that bend and sway, you point us to the holy way.
O Christmas tree, O Christmas tree, you point the way to glory!

Mark A. Rideout

Call to Worship · Isaiah 64:1–9

God has done many awesome works.
Mountains have quaked and waters have boiled.

We are not impartial witnesses—
we have seen miracles and have not been afraid.

God has given us this world, and even as we do wrong to it,
we are loved. We have a home.

We have seen God's patience.
We have felt unconditional love.

God works for those who wait and watch for signs,
for those who give tirelessly to others,
and even to those of us who struggle in trying to live God's word.
We have a duty to watch and to wait,
we have a responsibility to act, but each day,
we have the good fortune to live in the sight of God.

Opening Prayer

In your love, God, we have become your family. When you sent the world a teacher in Christ, we did not know that we were his sisters and his brothers. We did not understand the significance of our new place. You have adopted us, taken us in, so that even those who do not know mother or father or sister or brother on earth may have you, so that each one of us can be part of the same family, so that neighbors and enemies all may have one blood and one understanding of peace. We are so lucky, God, to call you Mother and Father, our Protector and Redeemer. Amen.

Confession

God, we often discover ourselves lost in the wilderness. We have made our choices, and chosen wrong, and the result is a long, lonely, terrifying journey in a cold land. We have neither mother nor father there, we can find no friends save the voices of those we have left behind. We are afraid, and we call out for your love. Forgive us, God! And lead us back to your grace. Amen.

Assurance of Grace

God hears all our prayers, even those that come from afar. Have faith and rejoice in the forgiveness we find there.

Unison Prayer

God, you are eternally faithful. As we wait and watch, housed here in the wonders of your world, we are struck again and again by how remarkable this faith is. You have given us all we can see and taste and feel, and, still, it is not enough—still, you give more. You listen when we call out to you, our mouths dry and dusty with the dirt of the many hard roads we travel. You speak to us with holy breath; you guide us into the arms of those who can care for us. You are, truly, our most steadfast friend, and we give thanks. Amen.

Maria I. Tirabassi

Call to Worship

Come to worship: Shouting!

God lives and moves among us!

Come to worship: Singing!

Mary invites us to join in her lullaby.

Come to worship: Praying!

We offer our confessions, petitions, and praises.

Come to worship: Listening!

Today may our ears be opened to new understanding of your story.

Jacqueline A. Burnett

~

OPENING WORDS FOR CANDLE LIGHTING SERVICES

Advent 1

prophets past & present

The first candle honors the earth, from which we are all born; the bed of straw on which the Child will lay; the many roads he will walk, beginning with the road to Bethlehem, which he travels in his mother's womb. May this candle waken our longing for Christmas.

Advent 2

the journey to Beth.

The second candle honors water, in which we all are brought to life. It honors the water that cradled the Child in Mary's womb and the water of the river Jordan in which Jesus was baptized. It honors the Sea of Galilee that filled fishing nets for him and the Sea of Tiberius that will let him walk upon its waves. It honors the well of Jacob, where Jesus gave himself as living water to a woman in need. May this candle waken in us our thirst for Christmas.

Advent 3

Shepherds who.

The third candle honors air, the breath of life by which we are kept in life. It honors the atmosphere in which the Child grows—the blessings of angels and the love he knew from his parents. It honors words of wisdom that come from the magi and heartfelt questions that begin with shepherds and keep on coming from ordinary folks even now. May this candle waken us to the deep, clear breath of Christmas.

Advent 4

angels

The fourth candle honors fire, the warmth of life that keeps us alive. It honors the Star of Bethlehem, shining on the Christ Child in the hay, and angel light that brings shepherds to the stable. It honors the seaside fire on which Jesus will cook breakfast for his friends at Easter and the fire of love burning within their hearts for him, even in death. May this candle waken in us a burning desire for Christmas.

Christmas Eve

The Christmas Candle honors the Child, who warms and lights our lives, who refreshes us with stories and waters us with promises, and whose fruitfulness we hope to be. It honors ordinary and powerful people, Christmas creatures and a Star, who found in the Child a love worth remembering. It honors flowing rivers and teeming seas that lent their power to him, and an ocean of human souls who have flowed to him over the centuries. May no heart be untouched this night, and may every wandering soul find a way to Bethlehem.

Nancy Rockwell

Christmas Gloria (traditional tune of "Gloria Patri")

Glory be to the Christ Child,
God's strength made weak, has come to light our way.
As the first born of creation, the Alpha and Omega,
Won-der-ful birth, God has come to earth.

Jacqueline A. Burnett

Call to Worship

There are many questions—even the sure among us
have hearts that are filled with doubt.

**We must stand together, here,
within the small circle of these lights.**

We so often feel alone, unappreciated, or neglected.
Tasks we once performed with joy are now resented.

**Within the circle, there are many hearts, many hands to hold,
many with problems greater than our own
who need our love and support.**

Some days it is hard to stand apart from the spirit.

**When we step into the circle,
when we allow ourselves to reach farther
toward others who are hurting,
we will never be apart from the spirit.**

Maria I. Tirabassi

listening with my eyes
i see you in beauty
i hear beauty in all of its ways
splashing colors upon my palette
flashes of light from within from without

you surround me
listening with my heart
i search for you in love among all
i walk with
a sign a spark of heaven here
in the in between
in some sign of need
some outstretched hand
or call for compassion

listening with my soul
i search for you
beyond the light beyond the image
beyond the seen or heard
in a knowing
to rest in
the moment of no thing
that lies before creation
in my poverty
my joy

Susan Morse

Confession (any Sunday in Advent)

Birther of Our Lives, in this time of preparing, we struggle to make time for your coming. When there are presents to get, we forget your presence among us. With "so much" to do, we forget the mystery of your Being and the miracle of our being avenues of your grace. Slow us down. Loosen us up. Let us laugh at ourselves more freely and love each other more generously. In the midst of the tinsel and the bustle, help us see the twinkling joy. In the name of the One Whose Being Blesses Humanity, Amen.

Assurance of Pardon

Beloved, hear the words of grace. The glory of God shone around the shepherds on a "normal" night. The angel telling them not to fear spoke in the middle of a regular work week. Love comes to us that our common lives may become God-stained with joy. Let us rejoice, truly believing we are forgiven.

Priscilla L. Denham, Confession; MCT, Assurance

Hope of All Nations, we come here seeking to know your way to peace and goodness. You made us strong that we may work for you; meek that we may know our need of you; full of joy that we may sing praise to you; empty that we may receive you. Come to us, Christ Jesus. Amen.

Kathryn J. Campbell

Opening Prayer

Thank you God, for each person we see here today. Every one of us has taken a moment away from the concerns and fun of the holiday season to center ourselves, to regain perspective on the season. Each of us has found comfort here and chooses that comfort over a schedule that leaves no time for ourselves. We are blessed. We are lucky to stand witness for each other, to give testament in smiles, conversation, and prayer. These faces will stay with us, God, through the rest of our week, through all of our decisions, and they will remind us to keep our hearts filled to the brim with your loving grace. Amen.

Confession

It is difficult during this season to find time for others, God, even when we tell ourselves that all we do is for them. We forget that what our family needs is our time, not our presents, that what they want from us is love, and not money spent. It is selfish of us, but we hide behind lists, denying them the gifts they really want. Amen.

Assurance of Grace

God always surprises us with forgiveness. Let us surprise ourselves, truly—let this be time when we share the best parts of love, compassion, joy, and peace.

Invitation to Offering

God gladly meets us half way when we remember to do good works. Every time we offer up our gifts, we are sharing in that wondrous gift we have been given in Christ.

Dedication

When we have drowned ourselves in sin, God has forgiven us. When we turn our faces from God's healing, we are not thrust away. And when we do as much as we can to help others, our generosity does not go unnoticed. Thanks be to God!

Maria I. Tirabassi

BLUE CHRISTMAS SERVICE

Words of Welcome

Welcome to the Blue Christmas Service. We are pleased that you have joined us for this service, when we recognize that, for many, Christmas is anything but merry. We acknowledge that the holiday season can be difficult for those of us who are grieving the loss of loved ones, who have difficult family relationships, who struggle with addictions, physical and mental illness, depression or stress, and who feel deeply the pain of those in our world who suffer the effects of war, poverty, and disease. So we gather together as a community to express and acknowledge these conflicting emotions, as we remember that it was into such a world as this that God's love took on flesh in Jesus, our Redeemer.

Call to Worship

In the midst of this season when we celebrate the hope of Christ's coming, we come together to share our grief.

The Word became flesh and lived among us, full of grace and truth.

In the midst of this season when we celebrate the peace that Christ brings, we come together to acknowledge our pain.

All who receive Christ are given the power to become children of God.

In the midst of this season when we celebrate the joy of Christ's coming, we come together to name our fears.

What has come into being through Christ is life, and that life is the light of all people.

In the midst of this season when we celebrate the love that Christ brings, we come together to be upheld in our struggles.

The light shines in the darkness and the darkness will not overcome it.

Let us worship Emmanuel, God with us, in the midst of all the celebration and sorrow of this season.

Invocation

God of love and comfort, who promises us an end to all mourning, crying, and pain, be present with us now as we bring our struggles before you. As you became flesh, experiencing all the grief and joy of being human, living and dying among us in this troubled world, send now your Holy Spirit, our Comforter, to hold us in your love as we acknowledge all the complex emotions that this season brings. With the lighting of these candles, may the light of your presence shine among us and warm the bleak midwinter of our hearts. O come, Emmanuel, and fill the whole world with heaven's peace. Amen.

Lighting of the Advent Candles

During the season of Advent, we use the Advent wreath and the lighting of candles to help us mark our weeks of expectant waiting. We await the celebration of Christ's coming into this world on Christmas and we await the time when Christ will come again, making real God's promised realm of peace. Throughout Advent, when we light these candles, we proclaim the coming of the light of God into the world with messages of hope, peace, joy, and love.

Today (tonight) we take a moment to recognize that this time of expectant waiting is complex and conflicted, that the cry, "O come, O come, Emmanuel" is sometimes filled with anguish and grief for those who are desperately in need of God's presence. We use the same Advent wreath and the lighting of candles to acknowledge the grief, pain, fear, and struggle that are also part of this season. With the lighting of candles, times of silent meditation, words of scripture, and singing, we bring all of these things before God, knowing that God has promised to be present with us when we gather together in God's name.

During the time of meditation, we encourage you to pray for the people and situations in your life and in our world that are in need of God's presence. We also encourage you to write down these prayers using the paper and pencils in your pews. At the end of the service, there will be a time when you are invited to bring those written prayers forward, leaving them here in this sacred place, as a symbol of your desire to share the weight of the burdens they represent with God and with this community.

Sing "O Come, O Come, Emmanuel" (verse 1)

First Candle—Grief: We light the first candle to share our grief: grief over loved ones who have died, over relationships that have ended, over the many kinds of loss we have experienced. Often it is during these special holiday times, these times that are filled with memories, that we feel most deeply the absence of those we have loved and lost. May this candle bring to light our grief.

Silent meditation

Read John 11:32–35

Sing "O Come, O Come, Emmanuel" (verse 2)

Second Candle—Pain: We light the second candle to acknowledge our pain: the pain of addiction; the pain of physical or mental illness; the pain of troubled relationships; the pain of depression—all the pain and burdens that we experience. In the midst of the joy of the Christmas season, we sometimes feel the need to hide the pain that we feel so that we won't burden others. May this candle bring to light our pain.

Silent meditation

Read Matthew 11:28–29

Sing "O Come, O Come, Emmanuel" (verse 3)

Third Candle—Fears: We light the third candle to name our fears: fears of uncertainty, fears of being alone; fears of those who are not like us or whom we don't understand; fears of change or stagnation—all the fears that hold us back from living life to the fullest. Just as the shepherds, wise men, King Herod, Mary, and Joseph were filled with fear that first Christmas, so we too live in a world and a time that is filled with fear. May this candle bring to light our fears.

Silent meditation

Read Isaiah 41:8–10

Sing "O Come, O Come, Emmanuel" (verse 4)

Fourth Candle—Struggle: We light the fourth candle to recognize the struggles of our world: the struggles of those who suffer the effects of war; the struggles of those who need food and shelter; the struggles of those who are fighting to survive diseases like AIDS and illnesses like cancer; the struggles of those who long for freedom from oppression; the struggles of those who are experiencing all that we have already named. We know that our own struggles are part of the struggles of a world desperately in need of God's promised realm of peace. May this candle bring to light our struggles.

Silent meditation

Read Revelation 21:1-6a

Sing "O Come, O Come, Emmanuel" (verse 5)

Time of Remembrance and Prayer

We invite you now to say aloud or bring forward the prayers that you have written, as a symbol of your desire to share the weight of burdens they represent with God and with this community. Leave them here in this sacred place, in the presence of God and God's people, knowing that you and your prayers are held in the arms of God's love.

Lighting the Christ Candle

In the midst of all that we have shared, acknowledged and named here, God is with us. We light this candle to remember that God has come and is coming into the world. The Light that is the life of all people shines, here and now, among us.

Scripture reading: John 1 (selections)

Sharing the Peace of Christ

Jesus said to his disciples: "Peace I leave with you; my peace I give you. I do not give to you as the world gives. Do not let your hearts be troubled and do not let them be afraid." As Jesus shared these words of peace and comfort with his friends, so we invite you to share words of the peace of Christ with those around you.
The peace of Christ be with you.

And also with you.

Sharon N. Fennema

Opening Prayer

Please God, in this moment, give us rest. Allow us to open ourselves to you, to let you see the best and the worst of our decisions without fear of your judgment. Help us to set down and rest from the worries of this season. We cannot fix every problem. Nothing will be perfect, but you will still love us. As your children, we are not expected to perform miracles in our daily lives—not even at Christmas. All you ask of us is that we share of ourselves with those who need help, that we listen when another is brave enough to speak, and that we don't allow fear and anger to color our actions. Thank you for the joy you offer, even in the face of all that a frustrating world can throw at us. In your name we pray, Amen.

Maria I. Tirabassi

How Beautiful . . . · Isaiah 52

How beautiful upon the mountain
    are the feet of them that preach
How beautiful upon the coastal plains
    are the toes of those who teach
How lovely beside the French Broad riverbank
    are lips that sip
        new figures of speech
How sensuous the writer's pen
    that dreams of presidents
        to impeach
I beseech you, brethren, ignore this
    sad and baneful breach
        of good poetic judgment
And consider how beautiful
    are your own sweet feet
        upon this mountain—
    how good news is made manifest
        in *each* of you
        who are gospel, who bring glad tidings,
        who proclaim salvation, now within reach . . .

Abigail Hastings

Invitation to Offering

We have been blessed many times over, and when we do God's work with a glad heart, it is a blessing unto itself.

Dedication

There are many ways we can offer our thanks for the gifts we receive. We choose to show our gratitude, for when we are lost, God returns us to the fold, and when we have given up all hope, we are redeemed.

Call to Worship

The new year is nearly upon us.

There are promises yet to fulfill.

Very soon, we will burst into a new season of grace, free once more to commit to joy, excitement, love, and forgiveness.

We are lucky to see each day and each year as a cup overflowing.

Praise God for the blessing of a heart that always struggles to renew!

We are blessed to meet this season with a spirit that has learned from the past and yet yearns toward the future. We are thankful!

Opening prayer

A new year is upon us! In these dark days, we struggle to make light with new resolutions. We warm ourselves by a fire stoked with possibility. We are half afraid of it, of how hot we can burn when we are ignited by fresh hope. We are dazzled by how bright our lives could be, so much so that we often turn away too soon. God, be with us as we find a way to make these possibilities our own. Help us to walk forward with confidence in all we are capable of. God, remind us that our potential may become a reality. Amen.

Maria I. Tirabassi

NATIVITY CYCLE OPENINGS

Advent 1: Mary Hears from God

We are waiting. We are frustrated and tired. So much of our world seems caught in turmoil. Many are dying of AIDS as well as terrorism. The darkness closes in on us. Where is the hope?

In the darkness God lights the first candle of Advent.
The divine word is sent to a young teen in a little land in the Mideast.
"I'm going to bring a new life into the world, to bring about change, to offer love and salvation." What will be her answer? We listen with bated breath.

"Let it happen as you say, O God. May the fruit of my womb bring good news to us all."

Light candle

Prayer: As you brought the word of hope to Mary and through her to our world, rekindle anew in us this season a sense of hope as we prepare to celebrate your nativity. Amen.

Advent 2: Joseph Must Decide What to Do

Light first candle

We are still waiting. One candle in the darkness doesn't offer much light. And with a promise to act comes responsibility to respond. Taking a risk in a threatening world goes against our need to run and hide.

Poor Joseph, caught in a dilemma. Do what society expects and distance yourself from what might appear scandalous. Or stick by the frail child facing pregnancy. What will his choice be?

"Mary, I'm here. We'll go through this together." A second candle now flickers in the darkness.

Light second candle

Prayer: It takes courage, O God, to stand with those who would do your work. May we find the strength to offer our support to your good news. Amen.

Advent 3: An Innkeeper's Hospitality Issue

Light two candles

The Christmas season is filled with activities—shopping, partying—added to our normal flow of things. How can we find time to entertain the Christ child? So often we go with what clamors the loudest, and we miss the gentle "tap tap" at the door.

Weary travelers choke the inn demanding their lodging, food, entertainment. And here stand a pair of poor ragged souls asking you to do even more. How can one be hospitable in such a time to such as these?

"I'm sorry, but I am full. But I see you too have need. Perhaps we can work something out. There is a stable out back . . ." And another candle joins those flickering two.

Light third candle

Prayer: O holy child of Bethlehem, we open our hearts to you. And we seek to offer your hospitality to others in need in this holy season. Amen.

Advent 4: Animals Must Share Their Manger

Light three candles

We often speak of shepherd and magi receiving the good news in this season, but they were not the first. Was it a cow or ox, donkey or sheep, who found its manger occupied with love incarnate?

The good news comes not just for humankind, but all of creation. Those representatives were there not just to be cute, but to remind us that all of God's world groans awaiting the good news. Are we as welcoming as these creatures who gave of their stalls?

"Baby Jesus asleep on the hay. We know about birth and caring for our off-spring. We know one needs a place of safety where one may curl and rest." Yet another light joins the fight against the night.

Light fourth candle

Prayer: The cattle are lowing; creatures are sharing their songs of parenting to welcome new birth. May we also welcome love's birth with our own sounds of support. Amen.

David Schmidt

Call to Worship · Psalm 89:1–4, 19–26

God, we know we should always speak the words of your mouth.

It is difficult, though, to remember how to tell of your steadfast love.

We should sing of joy, love, peace, and of Christ's coming to redeem us.

**It is easier to speak with the popular voice of our age—
it is easier to spread dissent than it is to share what really matters to us.**

You have given us your eternal faithfulness, God,
and we must find a way to sing with your tongue.

**We must let your words be ours, God,
and let your faith strengthen us
until we are strong enough to speak with our own grace.**

Maria I. Tirabassi

Lighting of Advent Candles—Fourth Sunday of Advent

Why have you come to this place and this time?

We come to worship and to wait, wait for the stirrings of new life.

What is it you want from your God?
We come hoping for hope, *(Light first candle)* praying for peace, *(Light second candle)* longing for love, *(Light third candle)* and dreaming of joy.

Have you heard the words of the angel?

We have heard. The herald told the most ordinary people,
"Behold, I bring you good news of a great joy
for all the people of the world." Today we almost dare to believe.
We light this candle that its light may reveal the coming of the light of God into the world. This light is joy, *(Light fourth candle)* joy that is ours, joy for the world, joy shot through the commonest of days all year. Let joy be real for us, in us, and through us. Amen.

Priscilla L. Denham

Call to Worship

This season, we have faced many challenges, and still more lay ahead.

We have been petty and spiteful, we have spoken without thinking, we have forgotten gifts and cards, we have too little time and too many obligations.

There is still much to be grateful for and there are many to remember.

There were quiet moments, those answered prayers
of health and vitality for our families and friends.

We have, each of us, held Christmas in our hearts, one way or another.
We have found peace, if only for a moment.

This year and next, we will ask more of ourselves—
more time for rest, for laughter, for the grace of loved ones—
we will not just pray for peace, we will work for it.

Confession

We find, God, that we do not live every day as though it were a day of worship and reflection. We do not set aside time for ourselves, for the questions of our children, for the company of our elders. Instead, we allow the voices we love to be drowned out by the concerns of the week. We allow the prayers of our hearts to go unspoken and unheard. Amen.

Assurance of Grace

We never speak so softly that God cannot hear us. We never turn off our hearts so completely that God cannot remind us of what we truly need.

Maria I. Tirabassi

Advent Charge and Benediction

We have peeked at the light under the stable door.
Do you have the courage to unwrap the gift the Christmas Christ brings?
Go forth now and open the door to let joy break forth.
Open the gift and give hope to one another.
Open your heart and let peace and love enter in. Amen.

Jacqueline A. Burnett

2

A CLUTCH OF STARS

Words for Christmas

NOW TO GOD WHO IS ABLE TO
STRENGTHEN YOU ACCORDING TO
MY GOSPEL AND THE PROCLAMATION
OF JESUS CHRIST, ACCORDING TO THE
REVELATION OF THE MYSTERY THAT
WAS KEPT SECRET FOR LONG AGES
BUT IS NOW DISCLOSED, AND THROUGH
THE PROPHETIC WRITINGS IS MADE
KNOWN TO ALL THE GENTILES, . . .
TO THE ONLY WISE GOD, THROUGH
JESUS CHRIST, TO WHOM BE
THE GLORY FOREVER! AMEN.

Romans 16:25-27

Prayer of Invocation

God, Giver of every good gift,
We gather here by habit or by accident, from lives frantic or serene. We gather
here, young, old, in middle age, all of us children whose names you know by
heart. We gather here, each of us hoping for
    A new word
        A gentle touch
            A nudge in the right direction
                straight into the arms of love. Amen.

Molly Phinney Baskette

Gentle God, as we contemplate the dizzying contrasts of the past year, guide us to concentrate on the golden moments that illuminated our lives; the challenging hikes through your awe-inspiring wilderness, glimpses of exhilarating wildlife, quiet conversations, shared laughter, shared tears, warm embraces, and fish tacos. Thank you for including us in your crazy creation. Amen.

Susan Hodge-Parker

Call to Worship—Christmas Eve or Christmas Day   ·   Luke 2:8–20

Through lush farmland and bleak alleys

sweeps good news of great joy!

Through empty wants and desperate needs

blazes a star to light our way.

Through pounding turmoil and dazing fear

sounds an angel chorus:
Glory to God in the highest;
peace to God's people on earth!

Receive the news! Follow the star! Heed the angels!

Through song and silence, word and wonder,
let us make our way to Bethlehem.

Let us worship the Holy One
who beckons in an infant's cry.

Ann B. Day

nice prayer

Christmas   ·   Genesis 1 & 2, John 1:1–4, 9, 12, Matthew 5:16

Holy One, you gave us the gift of life, you put us in a stunning world, and you made us free to choose. In Jesus Christ, the Light of the World, you gave us new life and new hope for knowing you. May that Light shine through our choices, our words, and our acts, so that others will praise you, source of Light and Love. Amen.

Kathryn J. Campbell

Prayer of the Downhearted at Christmastime

What do we do, God, when life does not go according to our plans—
when troubles come, or dreams are shattered and our expectations are denied?
Some of us are here feeling that this Christmas is the wrong festival at the
wrong time. What is there to celebrate?

We are like Joseph, perhaps—disappointed and embarrassed. That in which
we put our faith has betrayed us, like Mary when she was found to be expecting the unexpected. But you choose to bless us by putting the unexpected in our way.
Can we see your way—hold fast to your blessing? Can we hear your voice
calling out to us in love?

This child, whose birth we celebrate in the middle of winter, at the darkest
time of the year, was the One who grew up to say: "Come to me, all you
who are weary and burdened, and I will give you rest."
We hear the words of Jesus, O God, and find rest for our souls.

Ruth Richards

Lighting of the Advent Candles—Christmas Eve or Christmas Day

(* indicates lighting)

We have waited for weeks. We have waited all our lives for this time, this
blessing. This is when we pray our yes, like Mary. When we are finally ready
to have God enter into our lives, filling us with life that is ours.

**Like a new mother, we nurture this new life with hopeful belief*, peaceful
living*, loving care*, and joyful acceptance*. The Advent candles blaze,
symbolizing the light of these gifts in our lives.**

As we light the Christ candle* tonight for the first time, may it remind us that
Christ is the true center of our lives.

**Most gracious God, as we celebrate the birth of Jesus, may our lives become
centered on living in your hope, peace, joy, and love. Amen.**

Priscilla L. Denham

CHRISTMAS MEMORIAL TREE BURNING CEREMONY

Throughout Advent, place a small Christmas tree in a prominent place and leave a basket of blank strips of paper with a wire for attaching to the tree nearby. People write names of those they love who have died and hang them on the tree. This ceremony is for disposing, in a sacred manner, of the strips of paper after Christmas.

(Items needed: strips of paper with memorial names, burning bowl, copal or another kind of incense)

Reflection

Incense has been used in religious rituals for as long as human beings have known religion. The incense we are burning today is called "copal," from Mexico: it was used by the Aztecs in many of their purification rituals and is known in practically every continent in the world as an incense set apart specifically for religious purposes.

Ancient Judaism and early Christianity understood the smoke of incense to have certain properties that reflected and invited God. The Hebrew word for smoke, without vowels (as Hebrew is written), is precisely the same as one of the names for God. In addition, smoke has the property of being, like God, present but invisible/transparent. And the smoke of incense, in addition to bearing aromas that work on our moods and psyches, stays with us, permeating our hair and clothing, even after we leave the sacred space—just as we do not leave God behind when we depart from church, but take God into our very being to travel with us through our daily lives.

Let us remember these properties as we remember the people we have loved who have moved on to a new way of being today—that we will never leave them behind, because they permeate our memory.

Burning of the Paper

(Take each name off the tree in turn and say each aloud):

God abide with

And abide in us.

Closing Prayer

God with us, we have gathered here today with a sense of the sacredness of this space, a sense of the sacredness of our relationship to those we have lost from this life, and whom we now celebrate and remember.

As we leave this place today may we take into ourselves what is best of them, what is holy and good, that spark of Life that you gave to each of them and never took away, even when death claimed their bodies and led their beings back to you. In the name of Christ who conquered death and brokenness from God so that we would never truly die again, we pray, Amen.

Molly Phinney Baskette

Call to Worship · Jeremiah 31:7–14

God promised to gather us up, to bring us together,
although we may be scattered across the land.

We sing together the greatness of God.

God promised us comfort, a release from terror,
and a respite from the pain that follows us on earth.

We sit together, marveling at the abundance of God.

God promised that the people would be satisfied with this bounty.

We work together, that all people might share God's bounty.

Maria I. Tirabassi

Dedication

In simple trust we bring our gifts,
Our tithes of all we've known
We hear your calling in this hour,
Feel stirrings of the Spirit's power
Lift wings grown tired as stone.

To share our lives and spread the hope
Meant not for heaven afar,
But for your hurting and forlorn
Your child who wakened up this morn
Needing your love and ours.

Charlotte Hull Whiting

Manger Litany (with Open and Affirming Themes) · Luke 2

Amazing God, you love us so much that you came to us as an infant.

Born in a stable because there was no room at the inn.

You call us to love the world as we have been loved by you.

**Wrapped in swaddling clothes, you slept in a manger
because there was no crib.**

You command us to love our neighbors as ourselves

Shepherds welcomed you.

You call us to create an inclusive church
in which everyone is welcomed and loved.

No one was turned away from the stable door.

You keep calling to us to open our doors, to welcome the outcasts,
house the homeless, feed the hungry, and turn over the tables in the temple.

**Lambs and cows, chickens and donkeys, men, women, children . . .
angels of all kinds surrounded you.**

Help us create a world and a church in which all of your children are safe and
loved, affirmed, welcomed, and fully accepted, where we all have a community of angels surrounding us.

One star brighter that the rest led the world to your door.

May our love and work in the world be a beacon of hope to the hopeless, a
ministry of welcome for lesbian, gay, bisexual, queer, transgender, questioning, same-gender-loving, and heterosexual people. May our churches be
warm stables for all who have been hurt by homophobia and places of peace
and healing for all who have been wounded by violence. May we always seek
to make the powerful uncomfortable and accountable, especially when they
are us.

**Dear Child of Bethlehem, as we remember the stable and the manger, the
dusty roads you walked and the cross on which you died, give us the faith
and courage to tell your truth and make it our own. May your story guide
us and help us claim the sacredness in our own lives and stories. Help us follow you with all of our hearts and minds and souls and strength, for you are
our hope and redeemer. Amen.**

Frances A. Bogle

God of grace, lead us in this New Year to build new bridges. When discussion fails, help us to connect in other ways. Guide us to write a poem or a story, sing a lullaby or a love song, paint a picture, build an altar, plant a flower, create a dance, pray out loud, prepare a meal, or start with flour and yeast and bake the perfect loaf of bread. Grant us health, strong hearts, and clear minds. Amen.

Susan Hodge-Parker

Call to Worship · Galatians 4:4–7

Through Christ, we are one with God.
We are flesh and spirit, joy and sorrow.

We are more than what we seem.

Christ was God's gift to us,
and we celebrate always this gift of eternal grace.

We are redeemers and we are the redeemed.

We have received the most lovely gift,
and for that, we sing of a great song of peace.

**W have received it in order to go forth,
to share Christ's love with all who love to listen.**

Maria I. Tirabassi

A CRY IS HEARD: MOTHER REMEMBERS

(A monologue by Mary of Nazareth at age sixty)

This drama is dedicated to the memory of many children killed in our community—those abducted and found mysteriously dead, those killed by "stray" bullets and those knifed in daylight, and children who die unjustly anywhere at any time. The original piece was written for a worshiping community in the Bronx, New York.

Possible introduction: Four children enter with candles, light the Advent wreath, and dance with bright streamers around a manger in front of the altar. They dance down the main aisle, then return to the altar, forming a circle around the manger with hands held and heads bowed before leaving.

Mary walks to the front of the church, looking at the manger, and may then walk around meditatively to gaze at any other images or references to Jesus if they are present in church windows, paintings, banners, an altar Bible, etc. Finally, she looks at the cross.

It does not seem like that long ago he was a child, lying here, only this big (*gesturing with her hands*). I know it was no place to give birth to a child, and at the time, I was a bit overwhelmed by the circumstances. Now the memories seem so sweet, so bittersweet, maybe, the images mellowing within me like a kind of poetry, bigger than the simple facts . . . holding the power of a myth. I remember the joy, the people who understood, the children who came to sing and dance to him.

"A sword will pierce your heart." Yes, I heard that, too, but I was young then, eager and willing. I could never have imagined what was to come. Not that I'm sorry, at least not for me. I wish there could have been another way. I miss him . . . don't you? (*She walks toward the congregation.*)

I've pondered these things in my heart for a long time now, telling those who could understand when the time seemed right, when I felt ready. You probably have read some of what I told his friends. I know that some have written down what they saw and remember and some of what I saw, a living testimony to what he did here with us.

There's something else I want to tell, something I've kept inside for at least forty years now, something that happened not long after his first year.

You've heard about the journey we took, Joseph and the baby and I, our journey out of the country when he was born, where his life was in danger. That was one of the most terrifying nights of my life! We gathered our clothes, a bit of food, and then ran for our lives. When we finally got away, out of the city where his life was in danger, we all stopped to rest.

It was then I heard the screams, children crying out. They were dying. You've heard their cries too, haven't you? The little ones suffering, dying . . .

Was that the first of the swords to pierce my heart, the cries of the innocent from down in the city? There is no reason, never was, never will be . . . nothing to justify that . . . and I wondered if it was all just to try to kill him, the Holy Child, the one they feared would have the power to make a change, to throw the powerful down from their thrones and lift up the poor.

Is that what scared them? Were they afraid of the power hidden in one of these ordinary-looking children of the poor? Then, without thinking—I mean it came from such a deep place inside—I said softly, as in a prayer, "Can this be worth it? Why did this child have to be born and cause all this pain?"

I could not bear the thought that so many were dying because of him, while we were escaping the danger and they could not. Then the baby, who was, as I said, less than two, touched my cheek, looking up at me as I held him in my arms. (I never imagined he heard and understood.) He said to me, "Mamma, my life is for them."

The words made no sense, this little one snuggled in my arms on that dismal night that was wrapped in the howl of children as if it were the howl of a fierce wind. I can still hear that dreadful music, can hear it right now . . . and I wonder, is it only memory or are the children still dying somewhere near here tonight? I hear so much, the memories, the words he spoke, the things I saw and kept in my heart, and sometimes it all blends with what I see around me, like part of a whole symphony of truth.

But what I still don't know is, (*Mary walks to the cross and looks at it*) was it true? Did he give his life for them? Did what he gave—his whole prophetic ministry, his courageous suffering, his passionate hope, did it make any difference?

Who was the little one who once slept so quietly in this manger, only this big? (*Motioning and gently rocking a imaginary baby*) What difference did his life make . . . ?

(Mary returns to her seat among the members of the congregation, still rocking an imaginary baby as she sits quietly. The congregation sings, "What Child Is This?" Afterwards, members of the congregation are invited to come forward to share brief reflections on Mary's question: What difference has Jesus' life made to them? (In some communities, it may be appropriate to invite several people to be prepared to share reflections at this point in the worship celebration.)

Christina J. Del Piero

3

AWASH IN THE LIGHT

Words for Epiphany

It is [God] alone who has
immortality and dwells in
inapproachable light, whom
no one has seen or can see;
to whom be honor and
eternal dominion. Amen.

1 Timothy 6:16

Opening Prayer for the Season of Epiphany · Matthew 2:1–12

O God, you made of one blood all nations,
and, by a star in the East, revealed to all peoples
the one whose name is Emmanuel—God with us.
Enable us to recognize your presence among us
so that we might proclaim the rich love of Christ
in ways that shed his light upon all the world. Amen.

Jamie Norwich McLennan

Confession and Pardon · 1 Corinthians 13:4–7

God of faith, hope, and love;
We confess that we do not put love above all things;
    we are not patient and kind;
    we are arrogant and envious;

we like to see our enemy fall;

we demand our own way and complain when we don't get it.

Forgive us, God, as we forgive others. . . .

Through your gracious love, our sins are forgiven.

Through your guiding love, we forgive those who have sinned against us.

Thanks and praise to God, our faith, our hope and our love! Amen.

Susan E. Brown

LITURGY FOR EPIPHANY

Call to Worship · Isaiah 60:1–7

Arise, shine; for your light has come,

And the glory of our God has risen upon us.

God has pity on the weak and needy;

God redeems their life from oppression and violence.

Precious in God's sight are the widows, widowers, and orphans of war;

Precious in God's sight are the addicted and confused.

Precious in God's sight are the abused and neglected;

Precious in God's sight are the poor and desperate.

Precious in God's sight are all who sit on the margins;

Precious in God's sight are all who long for justice.

The glory of our God will rise upon them.

The glory of our God will rise upon us all.

Invocation

God of kings and paupers, of the satisfied and the destitute, shine your light into this place. Be present as we worship and bring the gift of our praise, and go with us as we leave, so that your light may shine in our hearts always, illumining the way to your love. Amen.

Confession

God, who has pity on the weak and needy, we come before you admitting our brokenness. We confess that we have not been a source of light to those in desperate need of light, and we confess that we have run from your light, preferring to hide in the dark places of our own need. Have mercy on us. Lift up your eyes and look around. Shine the light of your love on us all, that we may reflect your light in the places of our lives. Amen.

Assurance of Grace

God indeed looks up and sees our need. In Jesus, God has shined the light of love on us all. In the warm glow of God's light, our path is illumined and we leave this place enabled to look up and see the need of those around us. For this great gift, we give thanks! Amen.

Call for Offering

As the magi of old, guided by a light in the night sky, brought gifts of gratitude to God, so we bring our gifts. May these gifts be a source of light to those in need.

Dedication

God of Light, we have been illumined by the glory of your presence and enlightened by the word of your grace. We see and have become radiant with your love. We dedicate ourselves and these gifts for service in the world. May we be beacons of love and justice in a darkened world, shining your light on the poor and needy, the victims of oppression and violence, and all living in dark places in need of your light. Amen.

Jeffrey S. Nelson

LEADER 1: Let us greatly rejoice in the Lord!
See what has happened!
Come, see with your own eyes!
God has sent a Child to us, a Child like no other:
He shall teach us the ways in which we should go;
he shall lead us in the paths of peace.

LEADER 2: See what has happened! Come and see!
God has sent to us a child just as special as any child.
He cries; he smiles; his parents love him tenderly.
He teaches us the wonder of each new day:
the warmth in his father's hands,
the tenderness in his mother's eyes,
the sunlight on the animals' fur.

LEADER 1: He shall be tender and strong, teaching us of God's love.

LEADER 2: He shall be hurt and shall weep; he shall celebrate and shall laugh.

LEADER 1: We can't yet imagine all that he will become.

LEADER 2: We can't yet imagine all that he will become.

LEADER 1: Praise to God for this special child come among us!

LEADER 2: Praise to God for all the children come among us!

LEADERS: Sing praises to God!

Jane O. Sorenson

God of wise fools and foolish sages, jolt us out of our boring, clockwork days. Remind us that you are walking with us along every unexpected twist in the road. Thank you for sending that old trickster, Coyote, to turn our comfortable state of misery topsy-turvy and startle us with hope and joy. Amen.

Susan Hodge-Parker

Collect for the Baptism of Jesus
Matthew 3:13–17; Mark 1:4–11; Luke 3:15–17; John 1:29–34

God of life,
who flows in us and through us,
cleanse our hearts, minds, and spirits.
May we be awash in the light
of your life-giving love,
through Jesus Christ our Savior.

Patricia Catellier

LITURGY FOR THE BAPTISM OF CHRIST · Mark 4:1–11
Call to Worship (from a full baptismal font) · Genesis 1:1–5

(*Dip your hand in the water*) The voice of God spoke over the waters,

And the voice of God said, "Let there be . . . and there was."

The voice of God said, "Let there be (*name those assembled*), and there were."

And it was good.

(*Dip your hand in the water*) The voice of God came from heaven,

Women: And the voice of God said, "You are my daughter, the beloved . . ."

Men: "You are my son, the beloved . . ."

All: "With you I am well pleased."

In the washing of the baptismal waters, we became light—light to the world.

And God saw that the light was good!

Invocation

God, who spoke words of love for Jesus at his baptism, and who yet speaks words of love for us at the font, be present. Speak to us anew this day that we may speak boldly of you in a world that desperately longs to be re-created in your love. Amen.

Confession   ·   Psalm 29

The voice of God is powerful; the God of glory thunders; the voice of God flashes forth flames of fire: Before this God, we humbly bow and confess that we have not lived in the freedom of our baptism. We have not loved God as God loves us; we have not loved our neighbors as we are bidden. As you ordered the chaos of creation, so order the chaos of our lives. Speak to us tender words of love and forgiveness. Amen.

Assurance of Grace

God speaks again and again words of love and forgiveness, "You are my son—my daughter—my beloved ones; with you I am well pleased." Hear these words and go in peace. Our sins are forgiven.
Thanks be to God!

Call for Offering   ·   Acts 19:1–7

The Ephesian disciples received the gift of the Spirit and so were gifted for ministry in the world. In baptism, we were so gifted, and, in turn, we offer the gifts of our labor for the good of God's creation.

Dedication

God of glory, in baptism we dedicate our lives to you and pledge to become your voice of love in the world. Hold us close in our baptismal vows as we bring ourselves, our time, and our possessions to you that they may be gifts of your love in a world in which your tender voice of love is often drowned out by voices of violence, hatred, and oppression. Use us and all we have to your glory. Amen.

Jeffrey S. Nelson

Call to Worship · Luke 4:16–30

LEADER: May God be with you.

ALL: And also with you.

LEADER: The Spirit of God is upon us!

WOMEN: The Spirit of hope and joy!

MEN: The Spirit of challenge and truth!

LEADER: The Spirit of God is upon us, because God has anointed us

WOMEN: To bring good tidings to the poor,

MEN: To bind up the brokenhearted.

LEADER: God has anointed us

WOMEN: To proclaim liberty to captives,

MEN: To comfort the afflicted and to afflict the comfortable,

ALL: To join our bodies with Christ in service and song.

LEADER: Alleluia! Come, Holy Spirit!

Rochelle A. Stackhouse

The book on the shelf said, "Do it yourself."
Perhaps it applies to furniture, or home repair, or making jam.
But Holy One, these I cannot do alone:
I cannot learn without a teacher;
I cannot teach without knowledge;
I cannot comfort without a tender heart;
I cannot sing without joy;
I cannot challenge without courage.

Jane O. Sorenson

We Are Salt and Light · Matthew 5:13–16

If the human body, body of blood and muscle, is to live, it needs salt.

If the body of Christ, body of peace and justice, is to live, it needs us!

If the earthly creation, bustling and blooming, is to flourish, it needs the sun's light.

If the new creation we are in Christ, is to flourish, it needs the Spirit's light!

Jesus says we are salt of the earth, light of the world.

Our faith, our love, our hope—essential as salt and light.

But if salt isn't salty?

It isn't what it's meant to be.

And if a light doesn't shine?

It isn't what it's meant to be.

Jesus says we are salt of the earth, light of the world.

Briny and bright, we are God's faithful people.
We shall be who we are meant to be in Christ:
a welcoming oasis,
a compassionate community,
a justice-making people.
giving glory to God!

Ann B. Day

Dr. Martin Luther King Jr. Day Prayer

God of all people, We come here as your church this morning to worship you in community. May we listen with our hearts as you call each of us by name ... as you speak in the silence, in song, in scripture, in a sermon this Sabbath morning. May we continue the legacy of Dr. Martin Luther King Jr. and others who have peacefully worked for justice and equality for all people. Forgive us for what we have left undone. Help us to become vessels of reconciliation and to recognize our responsibilities to fight racism, sexism, economic deprivation, environmental destruction, and injustice wherever it is. We share the same hopes, tears, laughter, and dreams with all humanity. May we respond to Jesus' prayer "that they may all be one." Amen.

Sue Henley

O Great Lover, we arise from our beds to come to this place for so many reasons. For many it is the tranquility provided in this place, a place of silence in our noisy and chaotic worlds. Then there are those for whom it is like the comfort and reliability of a soft heirloom quilt that enfolds us when we need relief from the dark and cold with the knowledge that it has been and always will be at hand when we need it. For some it is because we are so tired that we must rest for a while because our week has been so busy and labored. And for some it is because of the playfulness and the sheer joy that we experience when we are with these partners in faith. Whatever the reasons that we enter this place today, may they come together today in one great climactic event that reveals your divine love for all of us and for all the world. Amen.

Brian Dixon

Epiphany

Almighty God, who comes to us in the gurgles of a newborn child: as the wise ones did of old, we too wish to bring gifts. What would you ask of us? What can we bring to you?

Help us to ask this question each day, every day, for you come to us each day, every day.

Jane O. Sorenson

SEVERAL LITURGIES USING LECTIONARY TEXTS FROM YEAR B
1 Samuel 3:1–10; Psalm 139; 1 Corinthians 6:12–20; John 1:43–51

Call to Worship

God calls the young.

CHILD: Speak, for your servant is listening.

God calls the old.

ELDER: Speak, for your servant is listening.

God calls women.

WOMAN: Speak, for your servant is listening.

God calls men.

MAN: Speak, for your servant is listening.

God calls all—rich or poor, gay or straight, abled or differently abled, black, white, red, brown, yellow—God calls all.

ALL: **Speak, for your servants are listening.**

Invocation

Loving Seamstress, who formed our inward parts and knit us together in the womb: be present here and stitch us together in love. Let the fabric of our life together provide warmth in a cold world and protection for the weary. Amen.

Confession

Patient God, repeatedly—day by day, hour by hour, minute by minute—you call us to serve you. But increasingly your voice is drowned out by the noise we have created to isolate ourselves from you and those around us—the noise of our TVs, our iPods, and our surround sound systems; the noise of our political pundits, our marketing gurus, and even our own voices. Forgive us. Quiet us, God, and teach us to listen for your voice, that we may know ourselves in you, and know what you would have us be and do to your glory. Amen.

Assurance of Grace

Come to the quiet. There, God speaks to us, discerning our thoughts with love and compassion. Know that you are wonderfully made, and that God loves and forgives you. Amen.

Call for Offering

As the boy Samuel ministered to God with the whole of his life, so we now give of ourselves, our time, and our talents in service to God's creation.

Dedication

Loving God, you called Samuel, Philip, Andrew, Peter, and Nathanael to follow, and they answered with their lives, saying, "Speak, your servant is listening." Give us voice to your calling, that we may similarly accept your invitation and, like Philip, invite others to experience the love we know, saying, "Come and see." Use the whole of our lives to this end. Amen.

Deuteronomy 18:15–20; Psalm 111; 1 Corinthians 8:1–13; Mark 1:21–28

Call to Worship

CHILD 1: The fear of God is the beginning of wisdom; all those who practice it have a good understanding.

God's praise endures forever.

CHILD 2: Anyone who claims to know something does not have the necessary knowledge.

God's praise endures forever.

CHILD 3: But anyone who loves God is known by God.

God's praise endures forever.

ALL THE CHILDREN: Knowledge puffs up, but love builds up.

God's praise endures forever.

Invocation

Blessed God, we are nothing except that we are loved by you. Be present in this place and enfold us in your love that we may go from here humbled to serve.

Confession

Gracious God, it is our privilege to be in your midst praising you, but it is just such a privilege that often breeds arrogance rather than humility. We confess that too often we wear our church attendance like a badge of honor and our faith like a cloak of righteousness, standing in judgment of others who barely darken a church door or who find meaning in life elsewhere. Forgive us. Teach us the lessons of love and remind us that, for all our knowledge about the ways of faith, the most important thing is that we are loved by you. Amen.

Assurance of Grace

God does indeed love us passionately and completely, forgiving our arrogance and pretense. Go assured that you are loved and are thus empowered to love—passionately, completely, humbly.
Thanks be to God!

Call for Offering

There is one God, from whom are all things and for whom we exist, and one Lord, Jesus Christ, through whom are all things and through whom we exist.

Let us bring the bounty of our lives and share it with all, giving back to God that which is God's.

Dedication

There is one God, from whom are all things and for whom we exist, and one Lord, Jesus Christ, through whom are all things and through whom we exist. We give you thanks for gifting us with so much—our selves, our time, and our possessions—signs indeed of your love for us. Make us grateful and humble in our sharing of these gifts that others may see your love in us. Amen.

2 Kings 5:1–14; Psalm 30; 1 Corinthians 9:24–27; Mark 1:40–45

Call to Worship

NARRATOR: A leper came to Jesus, begging him, and, kneeling, he said to him,

LEPER: If you choose, you can make me clean.

NARRATOR: Moved with pity, Jesus stretched out his hand and touched him, and said to him,

JESUS: I do choose. Be made clean!

NARRATOR: Immediately the leprosy left him, and he was made clean. After sternly warning him, Jesus sent him away at once, saying to him,

JESUS: See that you say nothing to anyone . . .

NARRATOR: But he went out and began to proclaim it freely—for how could he keep from singing?

AMEN! Yes! How could he keep from singing!

(Perhaps sing the hymn "How Can I Keep from Singing.")

Invocation

Hear, O God, and be gracious to us! O God, be our helper! Come into our midst so that we may praise you and tell of your faithfulness. Amen.

Confession

Holy God, Naaman was an important man used to dealing with important people. When he approached the king of Israel with great riches, astride his horses and chariots, he was met by the servant of an important prophet with a simple command: "Go wash." Naaman was furious, as much for the slight as for the simplicity of the command. As with Naaman, God, so are we. Forgive our presumption. Open our ears to hear you, whether through the words of the important or the unimportant. For what profit is there in my death, if I go down to the Pit? Will the dust praise you? Will it tell of your faithfulness?

Assurance of Grace

Sing praises to God, O you faithful ones, and give thanks to God's holy name. God has heard us and has been gracious to us. God has turned our mourning into dancing. God has removed our sackcloth and clothed us with joy. So our souls may praise God and not be silent! How can we keep from singing?

Amen! Yes! How can we keep from singing!

Call for Offering

The psalmist gave thanks and sang God's praises; the leper gave thanks and proclaimed God's good works; so now we give thanks out of the bounty of our lives.

Dedication

We will extol you, O God, because we cried for help, and you healed us. In your mercy, you did not leave us in our prosperity, but called us out to share our wealth, our time, ourselves with others out of gratitude for your great love. Because of this, our souls praise you and cannot be silent. How can we keep from singing?

Yes! How can we keep from singing!

Amen.

≈

Hosea 2:14–20; Psalm 103:1–13,22; 2 Corinthians 3:1–6; Mark 2:13–22

Call to Worship

VOICE 1: Dear people, do you not know that you yourselves are a letter from God?

VOICE 2: A *love* letter from God!

Bless God, O my soul.

Voice 1: You were written on God's heart,

Voice 2: to be known and read by all.

Bless God, O my soul.

Voice 1: Dear people, do you not know that God is *your* letter, as well?

Voice 2: A *love* letter from you!

Bless God, O my soul.

Voice 1: Written not with ink, but with the Spirit of the living God.

Voice 2: Written not on tablets of stone but on tablets of human hearts.

Bless God, O my soul.

Voice 1: And God writes: "I will take you for my spouse forever, in steadfast love and mercy."

Voice 2: And you answer . . .

Bless God, O my soul.

Invocation

Divine Lover, come into our midst and seduce us with your love. Make us yours as you are ours.

Bless God, O my soul.

Confession

Gracious God, we are sinners and tax collectors, all, speaking the names of the other gods—the other Baals—in our world—wealth, power, prestige, sex, work, love, honor, happiness, contentment *(pause for individuals to silently name their Baals)*. Forgive us. Soothe our restlessness. Take us to be your betrothed in love and faithfulness. Teach us to call you, "My Beloved," and as far as the east is from the west, so put our sins far from you.

Amen.

Assurance of Grace

God is merciful and gracious, slow to anger and abounding in steadfast love. God does not deal with us according to our sins, nor repay us according to our iniquities. As far as the east is from the west, so far has God removed our sins from us.

Bless God, O my soul.

Call for Offering

Jesus said, "The wedding guests cannot fast while the bridegroom is with them," and neither can we. For the banquet, we bring the best that we have—ourselves, our time, and our possessions—and offer them for the delight of the guests.

Dedication

God of the feast, you provide a banquet of good things out of the abundance of your steadfast love, and so we are satisfied. For this abundance, we give you thanks and offer to you the gift of our whole lives, that the banquet may expand and others may be invited to feast on the boundless goodness you give to us.

Bless God, O my soul.

Deuteronomy 5:12–15; Psalm 8:1–10; 2 Corinthians 4:5–12; Mark 2:23–3:6

Call to Worship

Voice 1: Sing aloud to God, our strength! *(organ swell)*

Voice 2: Shout for joy to the God of Jacob!

Alleluia!

Voice 1: Raise a song! *(organ swell, different from the first)*

Voice 2: Sound a tambourine! *(shake tambourine throughout the words; one hit at the end)*

Voice 1: Sound the sweet lyre with the harp! *(harp or violin arpeggio)*

Alleluia!

Voice 2: For God brought us out of the land of Egypt with a mighty hand and an outstretched hand.

Voice 1: Therefore, let us observe the Sabbath and keep it holy.

Alleluia! Alleluia! *(coordinated chord with all the instruments)*

Invocation

Ruler of the Sabbath, come into our midst and bless our Sabbath observance with your loving presence.
Come among us, God.

Confession

Ruler of the Sabbath, you created the Sabbath as a way to remember your lavish love toward us and commanded us to keep it holy. But in our arrogance, we have focused on the command and so lost sight of you, or we have disregarded the command and have forgotten your love. Forgive us. Instill in us a desire for Sabbath rest and refreshment, that we may once again be surrounded by your love. Amen

Assurance of Grace

The disciples were hungry and were provided food; a man was sick and was provided health; the Sabbath was made for humankind, not humankind for the Sabbath. It is the nature of Sabbath rest to be reminded of God's saving love, and so we are.

Thanks be to God!

Call for Offering

Like the apostle, we carry in our bodies the life of Jesus—a treasure in clay jars—for the life of the world. Let us offer the treasure of ourselves and our possessions for the life of the world.

Dedication

Ruler of the Sabbath, in love your have given us a treasure in clay jars—the life of Jesus in our giftedness, our time, and our possessions—that you call us to use for the life of the world. We lay these before you on this Sabbath, pledging all to you and asking that you use these treasures to your glory and for the sake of your creation. Amen.

Jeffrey S. Nelson

RESOURCES FOR TRANSFIGURATION
Matthew 17:1–9; Mark 9:2–9; Luke 9:28–36

Opening Prayer

Every morning we climb from our slumber
and head into our closets to begin the transformation—
sometimes stockings and heels or ties and jacket.
We hide ourselves in the fabric of this world
through white lies and clenched smiles.
We "make nice" and "get by"
and hide ourselves in the fabric of this world,
and at the end of the day we come here to you.
We cast our cares upon you.
We share our burdens with each other
and strip away our callous, outer selves
knowing you see through our dim disguises.
Our hearts and souls lay bare before you, God.
Manifest your presence here.
Let your voice be heard in the silence of our spirits
and the roaring in our ears.
Let your acceptance and forgiveness waft over us like a warm breeze,
your calm and comfort envelope and cradle us,
your love fill us with joy so that our smiles shine bright,
your light gleam in our eyes that others may see you
in our hearts and in our actions.

Prayer in the Midst of the Service

God of the Mountaintops,
from up here you can see forever—
down onto fluffy white clouds,
down further to the patchwork fields below.
The air is so crisp and clean, a little thin . . .
Is that part of my giddiness?
I love you, Jesus!
When I am up here with you, everything is perfect.
When I am up here, with a new friend, or a longtime love,
everything else is so far away it doesn't matter.
But you are not just up here—
You are God of the Plains and God of the Valleys,

God of the Every Day.
You are still God when friends betray, careers collapse
when temptations' snares have me struggling
and I feel that I am below the bottom.
Help me realize you were there and
you carry me through, bringing me back
to the here and now.

Closing Prayer *(form circle)*

God, You called Moses to lead your people out of slavery, and a bush glowed.
You gave Moses the law, and his face glowed.
Spirit, you called Elijah home, and the chariot glowed.
Jesus, you brought Peter, James, and John up the mountain, and you glowed.
Glow through us, as we go through our valleys
that others may see you and find the way. Amen.

Kenneth C. Wells

Call to Worship and Invocation for Transfiguration or for a Music Sunday
Matthew 18:19–20; John 10:7–10 or Transfiguration Texts

Loving God, your people long for a sign that you have not forgotten them!

Shine among us! Fill our land with your radiant glory!

Merciful God, your people are parched from the heat of their own sin!

Flow among us! Flood all peoples with your grace and mercy!

Life-giving God, your people grow cold as the world's grief takes its toll on them!

Blaze among us! Set our hearts on fire with compassion!
Send forth your word and let there be light!

Holy and loving God, we boldly claim the promise of Christ that where two or three are gathered in that holy name, Christ is present. With Christ among us, we know the power of your love for us. With Christ among us, we see your glory in the faces of our brothers and sisters. With Christ among us, we believe we can do all things through love's strength at work in us. Free us now to be a people renewed by transforming love of the One who came that we might have life, and have it abundantly. Amen.

David Sickelka

4

MEET US IN THE SHADOWS
Words for Lent

"TRULY (AMEN) I TELL YOU, JUST AS
YOU DID IT TO ONE OF THE LEAST OF
THESE, . . . YOU DID IT TO ME."

Matthew 25:40

Ash-sifter

Ash-sifter stirring,
prodding dried soot,
turning burnt ember:
peer close the grey.

Lift carefully edgewise
as if it were precious,
charred letters fading
papered remains.

Show me what to keep
and how to let rise,
smoke column wafting
years and lives.

William B. Jones

Prayer for Illumination for Lent

Matthew 4:1–17; Mark 1:4–15; Luke 4:1–21

God of covenants,
We often move through our deserts and wildernesses unchanged.
Today let us hear your words in scripture and song
so that they move us
and change us.
May we come from our time of worship
with the same fire and passion
that burned in the life of Jesus
as he came out of his wilderness. Amen.

Jamie Norwich McLennan

Ash Wednesday

I hunger on this day
to remember fire
and an oriental phoenix,
gold, on an ancient crimson garment.

Ashes
remind me
of Hiroshima
and Bergen Belsen
and burnt children in Bosnia
and a shattered Dad
sitting by a cold stove
wishing for death.

Where is an enduring coal
to re-ignite the Spirit's possibility?
The soldiers, on a cold night,
must have had a fire
at the cross's foot.

In a dying Christ
the phoenix rises.
The flame
points toward resurrection.

Roger Robbennolt

Marked by the Cross (for Ash Wednesday)

Like those who have gone before
walking this road of Christian faith
this day, we too, wear the mark of the cross.
This mark is, perhaps, more public,
This mark is, perhaps, more confessing—
than other crosses that we wear throughout the year.
It is a mere mark, however gritty
a dirty smudge which is even more humbling
than other marks, than other crosses that we bear.

But as you wear your mark of the cross from this place this day
may you remember all that it represents.
As you wear the mark of the cross
may you be mindful of ways in which the cross has already marked your life
and may you find daily, through this Lenten journey,
ways in which God is calling you to share with the world
the love and forgiveness which you have already come to know
in the gritty, humble, dirty, sacred mark of God—the Cross.

As you go to wash this mark of grit and ash from your own body
may you be mindful of the one whose love washes over us.
may you center on the one whose body lived, died, and rose again.
may you focus on the one who offers to remove all stains.
may you breathe a breath of remembrance of the one who gives us life
and may you, having confessed again what separates you from God's love,
say a word of forgiveness even to yourself.

Perhaps you may ask a loved one to wash the mark for you
May you receive the word of forgiveness they offer you—
a sign of God's reconciling love at work in this world
a sign of how we need each other to give witness to grace itself,
and move us ever closer to God's heart.

Elizabeth A. Long-Higgins

∾

LENTEN SERIES, "A TIME FOR . . ."
Ecclesiastes 3:1–8 and weekly additional texts

Week 1: A Time to Be Tempted
Genesis 2:15—17, 3:1–7; Matthew 4:1–11

For everything there is a season, and a time for every matter under heaven:

There are times when we are filled with joy and hope,
and other times when we are sad and scared.

There are times when we laugh, and times when we weep.

There are times when we are confident and strong,
and times when we are unsure and weak.

In every season, steadfast God, you promise to be with us.

When we are tempted to despair,
turn us back to your enduring promise.

Loving and holy God, as we enter into the season of Lent, we consider what it means to be tempted. When we hear your words of faithful promise, but are tempted not to believe, forgive us. When we listen to voices of the crowd and the false promises of advertising, call us back again to your steadfast path. When we cannot quiet our minds or our lives long enough to be aware of your presence, invite us once more to pause in the green pastures and visit the still waters. Forgive us, God. Have mercy on us. And receive us into your light and love. In Jesus' name we pray. Amen.

Week 2: A Time to Keep Silence and a Time to Speak
1 Samuel 3:1–14

Holy God, you promise to speak to us in a still, small voice, but our world and our lives are so loud that we can't hear you. You offer a voice of reassurance and an invitation of welcome, yet we are too busy to receive your blessing. Too often we pour out our concerns to you, but do not pause long enough to listen for your reply. We may live side by side with our neighbors, but never take the time to really pay attention to their words. Forgive us, God. Help us to have the wisdom of Samuel and say, "Speak, God, for your servant listens." Amen.

Week 3: A Time to Forgive · Matthew 18:21–22

Peter asked Jesus, "How often should I forgive?"

Jesus answered him, "Not seven times, but seventy-seven times."

What do we do when someone has harmed us?

How do we begin to do the hard work of forgiveness?

Jesus encouraged Peter to remember that he had been forgiven himself.

Forgiveness is a gift that God gives to us.
Learning to share that gift of grace is the challenge of our lives.
We are asked to receive God's forgiveness and give it to others.

Loving God, you ask us to forgive, and at times, we find that excruciating. You tell us to be welcoming, but we are tempted to close our hearts and our doors. You encourage us to treat others as we would like to be treated, but it is easier to judge others instead. Forgive us, God. Remind us of your mercy that you are always ready to give to us. Help us to receive your grace so that we may share it with others. In Jesus' name, we pray. Amen.

Week 4: A Time to Care · Matthew 25:31–46

To the righteous, Jesus said, "I was hungry and you gave me food,
I was thirsty and you gave me drink."

The followers were confused. "When, God? When did ever we help you?"

To the others, Jesus said, "I was a stranger and you did not welcome me,
I was naked and you gave me no clothing."

They were indignant. "Surely not, God. We would never abandon you."

Jesus said, "Truly I tell you, what you do to the least of these, you do to me."

Whatever we offer to another, we are offering it to God.

God of love and mercy, we long to live as your people and share the compassion that you first give to us. So often we hesitate, afraid to reach out, to care, to go the second mile, to truly give of ourselves. Forgive us when our actions and our words hurt other people. Have mercy on us when we simply neglect one another or are too busy to notice the needs all around us. Open our eyes and our hearts so that we might recognize all the opportunities that we have to share your love and compassion. In Jesus' name we pray. Amen.

Week 5: A Time to Mourn · John 11:17–36

Jesus lived a very human life;
there were times of mourning and times of rejoicing.

Jesus celebrated the joy of friendship, love, celebration, and togetherness.

Jesus suffered the pain of loss, betrayal, rejection, and loneliness.

Jesus mourned the isolation of sadness, discouragement, and loneliness.

In our moments of joy, we can turn to God with thanksgiving.

In our times of need, we can lift up our prayers,
knowing that God hears us and understands.

Eternal God, you tell us that for everything there is a season, and a time for every matter under heaven: You are with us from the time we are born until the time that we die. As we go through our lives, we pass through many seasons and experience the ups and downs of life; there is a time to weep, and a time to laugh; a time to mourn, and a time to dance; a time to seek, and a time to lose; a time to keep, and a time to throw away; a time to keep silence, and a time to speak; a time to love, and a time to hate; a time for war, and a time for peace. Gracious God, in every time and season, remind us that you are with us. In Jesus name we pray. Amen.

Palm Sunday: A Time to Die · Matthew 21:1–14; Isaiah 50:4–9

For everything there is a season, and a time for every matter under heaven.

There is a time to rejoice. We give thanks to God for our many blessings.

There is a time to plant.
We ask God to help us share the seeds of hope, love, and peace.

**There is a time to speak and a time to keep silent.
We ask God for wisdom in our relationships.**

There is a time to weep. We ask for God's strength in difficult times.

**There is a time to mourn, a time to die, a time to be reborn.
We pray for God's grace for what we cannot always understand.**

Holy and gracious God, we give you thanks that you are the God of all seasons. When we are in the midst of joy, help us to remember to give you thanks. When we are confronted with hardship and loss, let us remember that you walk with us to give us strength. When there are moments when we simply cannot understand and are faced with the question "why," remind us to turn to you and listen for your comfort and reassurance. You sent us your Son Jesus to show us what a human life can look like when it is lived fully. Help us to follow in his way. Amen.

Easter Sunday A Time to Rejoice · Jeremiah 31:7–14; Matthew 28:1–10

Christ is risen! *Alleluia!*

Christ is risen indeed! *Alleluia!*

The stone has been rolled away! *Alleluia!*

Death has been defeated! *Alleluia!*

Christ comes to bring new life and hope! *Alleluia!*

Nothing can separate us from the love of Christ! *Alleluia!*

To God be the glory and honor,
let us rejoice and be glad and together all say . . .

Alleluia! Amen!

God of every season, we celebrate the resurrection of your Son. We wish that our lives would be filled only with times of joy and laughter and peace. But Easter can come only after Good Friday. We know that there are seasons of sorrow and weeping and war. If there are times when we are tempted to give up hope, remind us of your faithfulness. Help us to place our trust in you, who conquered both sin and death. God, have mercy on us. Transform us. Roll away the stones from our hearts. Help us to put our faith in you in all seasons, so that we can live as an Easter people and rejoice in the promise of resurrection and new life. In Jesus' name we pray. Amen.

Susan J. Foster

Invocation · Psalm 24:1; John 17:6

Loving God, the earth speaks and tells us it is yours. We look at Christ and remember we are yours. With acts of kindness, words of truth, and laughs of joy may we proclaim your rule. May your peace fall upon all peoples as a blessing. We ask as followers of Christ. Amen.

Kathryn J. Campbell

Call to Worship · Jeremiah 31:31–34

LEADER: Come to worship God, who is making a new covenant with us.

LEFT SIDE: "I will write my law on your hearts," God says.

RIGHT SIDE: "I will be your God. You will be my people," God says.

LEFT SIDE: We will not have to teach one another about God,

RIGHT SIDE: for we will all know God, from the greatest to the least.

LEADER: Come and worship God, who forgets our wrongs and forgives our sins.

Donald Schmidt

Opening Prayer for a Season of Sorrow
Genesis 18–21; 1 Samuel 1–2:21; Luke 1:5–57

Loving God, our faces are sometimes lined with worry,
our days full of stress and struggle.
Yet we come today,
grateful that in the midst of this crowded and troubled world,
children are still born and bring hope to us.
Surprise us now with your presence;
Renew our sense of wonder;
Keep us open to the gift of your spirit
present in our singing, praying, speaking, and living. Amen.

Jamie Norwich McLennan

Confession

Merciful God, your steadfast love and desire to forgive give us courage to face
the wrongs that we have done. We confess that we have broken our communities; we have turned away the stranger; we have forgotten to love the land.
We have pushed your priorities aside and refused to let your commandments
question what we do. Forgive us, we pray. Restore us to our rightful minds,
that we may walk with you in caring for your world and all its creatures, in
the name of Jesus Christ. Amen.

Kathryn J. Campbell

Confession and Assurance of Grace for Lent
Micah 6:8; Isaiah 12:2–3; Psalm 107:1–9; John 4:10–14

We are parched and thirsty due to our failures
to live as God has called us to live—
doing justice, loving mercy, and walking humbly with God.
God does not leave us to die of our thirst,
but promises to quench our thirst
if we will but confess our failures
and admit our need.
Let us pray . . .

Holy God,
our souls are thirsty by our own choice.

We choose to fill ourselves with things
that only increase our hunger and thirst.
We choose possessions over people,
arrogance over humility,
discrimination over justice,
violence over peace,
and hatred over love.
Our lives are left dry and cracked from our sin.
Forgive us, O God.
Wash us again in the healing waters of your love.—
Refresh us and empower us to live as your people—
with justice, mercy, and humility,
embodying the good news of Jesus Christ
in whose name
and through your Spirit we pray.

Silence for personal confession

Let your heart be washed anew
in the healing waters of God's love,
for the steadfast love of God endures forever.
Sisters and brothers,
through Jesus Christ our Savior
God forgives us of all our failures
and through the Holy Spirit
nourishes us into life. Amen.

Wesley Brian Jamison

Call to Worship

It's spring and a good time for emerging and arising.

It's Lent and a good time for changes and life-altering decisions.

As the snow recedes we see life altering all around us.

Crocuses appear, coloring and brightening the soggy grass.

So does the Wiffle ball and bat that were left outside last fall.

It's a time to remember the cycles of life,
and the long distances we travel.

It's a time that comes around to remind us
about whom we serve, and whose we are.

David Pendleton and Abby Joy Pollender

Journeying to Jerusalem

Lent—an invitation
to reflect, to reconsider,
to slow down, to discover.
Invited by Jesus
to join him on the journey.
Invited to humble ourselves.

Sometimes on that dusty road
I feel lonely, and am fearful.
What lies ahead?
Will I be able to withstand the challenges?
Will I be enough?
Will I respond with joy
to the blessings to be realized?

We are called forth
out of the winter of ourselves
to re-imagine our relationship with God.
On Ash Wednesday we are marked—
tagged as Christ's own;
humbled now, readied to be exalted
as we draw closer to that place called Jerusalem.

As the birds awaken in spring,
the bulbs and the buds break forth
and the animals stir, so too we are roused.
We enter the city triumphantly,
having discovered that we are whole,
loved, perfect,
now, and always.

Gay Williams

Invocation · Psalm 92:1–3, John 3:1–16

Author of Life, you meet us in the shadows and protect us. You dance with us in the sun. You give us the breath of life and offer us eternal life. In this time of worship, open our hearts, our minds, and our hands so that we may love you and your creation in the way that Jesus did. Amen.

Kathryn J. Campbell

LENTEN CANDLE LITURGY

There are seven candles—one for each Sunday in Lent and one for Good Friday. Each week begins with one less candle lit, and extinguishes another. On Easter Sunday the darkened candles will be relit.

First Sunday

Meditation: We have come together this morning for renewal—in worship and as a community of faith. We've greeted one another, laughed, and hugged. But now the time of reflection and stillness is upon us. It is the first Sunday in Lent—the season for journeys of the heart. Close your eyes. Be still. Listen. We are entering a holy time. The Lenten candles have been lit, but over the next six weeks the light will slowly fade into darkness, for we are retelling the story of Jesus' betrayal and suffering and death. We do this not to be morbid, but because in the story of Jesus' death and resurrection, God is revealed—in the amazing transformation of death into life, in endings transformed into beginnings, and in dead-ends that become a source for new possibilities.

This is the sacred center of our faith—the truth made manifest in Jesus Christ—that God is in each and every one of us, quietly transforming us and the world. In his pain and suffering, Jesus speaks to every pain and loss you have endured and offers you the promise of transformation. It's an old story, but it still has the power to reveal, to heal, and to redeem. Jesus is at the heart of our faith, in the depth of our souls. He is waiting for us, inviting us to leave ordinary time and follow along with him on the journey that brought him to the Cross. Listen in silence, for Jesus is calling you.

Silence

As we extinguish this light, we acknowledge the darkness and pain of injustice in the world. *Extinguish candle.*

Loving God, as we journey through this holy season of Lent, give us strength and courage to make the changes that are needed in our lives. Open our hearts and minds to your steadfast presence and help us to put our trust in you. Amen.

Second Sunday

Meditation: On Sunday morning, for a brief space of time, we leave behind the world of home and work and school—the world where we have our lists of things to do, activities to participate in, tasks to complete. We come here this morning seeking something else. We come here seeking a shift—from the ordinary to the sacred, from doing to being. I invite you to close your eyes. Let go of your list. Recall that it is the season of Lent. Remember the parable of the sower. The sower throws the seed . . . and where it lands determines if it will grow or not grow. Think of it this way: think of the season of Lent as the sower, the time when seeds of faith are thrown with special intensity, as a time a time when God calls to us in a low, urgent voice. Listen. Jesus is being drawn inexorably to Jerusalem. Where is God calling you? What is God calling you to do?

Silent time

As we extinguish this light, we acknowledge the darkness and pain of prejudice and discrimination in the world. *Extinguish candle.*

Loving God, as we journey through this holy season of Lent, may we be open to your presence. Give us the strength to make the changes that are needed in our lives and the courage to take on the work of transforming the world. Amen.

Third Sunday

Meditation: There is so much during the day that clamors for our attention—friends, family, work, classes, household tasks. And the noise! We are bombarded with sound, from the clock that awakens us to the telephone, the radio, the television, the conversation that we have or overhear. Where is the time and place to listen for the still, small voice of God? Sometimes it seems that God would have to speak in a whirlwind to be heard above the clamor! Listen now. There is a place of quiet rest, and it is the place where God dwells within you. Close your eyes. Be aware of the place. In Lent we journey to the parts of ourselves known only to God, beneath the clamor. Let the story of Jesus reach us there. Let it teach us wisdom in our secret hearts.

Silence

As we extinguish this light, we acknowledge the darkness and pain of violence in the world. *Extinguish candle.*

Draw us together in your love, O God. May our restless hearts not resist you, but continue to search until they find their rest in you. We pray in Jesus' name. Amen.

Fourth Sunday

Meditation: It's Sunday morning. Last week, with all its demands, is over. The coming week, with yet another round of challenges and demands, is not quite here. I invite you to close your eyes and be in the moment. No matter where you are in your thoughts and feelings—relieved about what you have accomplished, anxious about what's left undone, concerned about people or projects—no matter where you are in your journey this day—I encourage you to set all that aside and consider where you are right now. Whatever is true for you right now, in this moment, whether it be joy or sadness, gratitude or anxiety, let it come forward. When it is fully present, then listen . . . for God is present in these moments, too. God meets you where you are and calls you forward, moment by moment, guiding you slowly but surely toward transformation.

Silence

As we extinguish this light, we acknowledge the darkness and pain caused by the lack of basic needs—lack of food, of shelter, of education, of health care, of love. *Extinguish candle.*

Loving God, we thank you that you are with us, and that we may call upon you no matter where we are, or what we are feeling. Keep us mindful of your presence and trusting in your promise—that you are working with us in the moment-by-moment unfolding of our lives. Amen.

Fifth Sunday

Meditation: When we arrived this morning we entered into the normal bustle of a church on a Sunday morning: friends greeting each other, choir members getting their robes, children bringing their energy and enthusiasm. Now that we are sitting together in the pews, I invite you to close your eyes . . . and consider the word, "sanctuary." A sanctuary is a place set aside for sacred things. It is a place of refuge and protection. This room is a sanctuary. The season of Lent is a kind of sanctuary, extended in time. And one of the things Lent teaches is that you, too, are a sanctuary. There is inside you a place for sacred things, a place where God abides.

Silence

As we extinguish this light, we acknowledge the darkness and pain of war, of persecution and oppression in the world. *Extinguish candle.*

Loving God, we open our hearts to you. We invite you into our inmost being, only to find you already there. Strengthen us in our quiet places and then lead us into the work of justice and peace. Amen.

Sixth Sunday—Palm Sunday

Meditation: We have gathered here, week after week, sharing a common quest for a deeper faith and a deeper experience of the divine. I invite you now to close your eyes and let go of the things that distract and concern you. Listen! The time is drawing near. Jesus is preparing to enter Jerusalem. How will we greet him? Will we follow him all the way to the cross? There is no deeper mystery than this: that the light came into the world, became flesh, and dwelt among us. The light of the world is going out. What will we learn this year in the dark night of the soul?

Silence

As we extinguish this light, we acknowledge the darkness and pain of illness and disease in the world, in body and in mind. *Extinguish candle.*

Loving God, there are so many choices before us every day—choices offered by our friends, our families, our culture, our own past. Some of them encourage the well-being of the earth, ourselves and our neighbors; others are destructive. Help us to distinguish between them. May we learn from the choices of Jesus and embody compassion, justice, and inclusion in all we say and do. Amen.

Good Friday

Meditation: Never doubt the meaning of Lent. It happened a long time ago, but it happened. Jesus walked on this earth. He practiced a ministry of radical inclusivity, drawing to himself all the despised and rejected members of society. He lived what he taught: a life of justice and love, of profound compassion for all people. He lived a life acceptable to you, O God. His death terrifies us, because it reveals how committed the world is to its own way, and the price the world exacts from those whose commitment is to you.

Silence

As we extinguish this light, we acknowledge the darkness and pain of all the children in the world who suffer in body, in mind, or in spirit. *Extinguish candle.*

What we contemplate this night is beyond words, beyond understanding. May the Holy Spirit intercede for us and give voice to what, for us, is inexpressible. Amen.

Easter

Proclamation: The light that the world tried to extinguish cannot be put out. Today we light the candles again, proclaiming the transforming power of God. As the light returns, we give thanks that God's transforming love has been, is now, and will ever be at work within us. Today we celebrate: new life, new joy, new possibilities. Christ is alive and living among us!

As we light the candles, we acknowledge that there is still pain and suffering in the world, but we place our trust in God and in the way shown by Jesus Christ. In the midst of darkness, there is light. In the pain of death, there is life. In the face of what appears to us to be overwhelming odds, God is at work in us and in the world for justice and peace, compassion and love, and life abundant. Christ is risen; Christ is risen in us, for wherever we gather in his name, he is there.

Relight candles.

Alleluia, Christ is risen; Christ is risen indeed!

Jeanyne Slettom

Lent/Easter Poem   ·   Matthew 21:1–11, 26, 27, 28:1–10

We want to share your resurrection glory.
We want to be part of the resurrection story.
But the cost for us seems much too high.
We don't want to suffer and die.

You overcame temptation and hate.
Your love for us determined your fate.
How can we understand love so strong?
Love that brought death for doing no wrong.

Hosannas were heard when they came to greet you.
Palm branches waved as they came to meet you.
But this earthly praise would not last long.
And soon they'd sing a very different song.

Your blood was spilled. Your body broken.
"King of the Jews," in derision spoken.
They nailed you to a cross on a hill.
You died. The heavens roared. Then it was still.

They placed you in a tomb that day.
But angels rolled the stone away.
And when the women sought you there,
They were distraught and in despair.

When you were not found in the tomb that morn.
The disciples scattered, lost and forlorn.
Then they saw you, but didn't understand.
Not even when they touched your wounded hand.

You suffered and died that we might live
You gave everything you had to give.
But hatred and death would not triumph o'er love
You were resurrected and returned to God above.

Now let us remember all the year through
That your love was not meant just for a few.
It's our duty and privilege to share it with all
Until that day when we receive heaven's call.

We get weighed down with our own stones and crosses.
We make money and possessions our lords and bosses.
Free our hearts for love as we tell everyone
We have been saved by the resurrection of God's Son.

Mary Taylor

Hymn—Forty Years the People Wandered
Matthew 4:1–11; Mark 1:12; Luke 4:1–13

(tune—"Beach Spring")
Forty years the people wandered, searching for their Promised Land,
Drinking water from the rock, and eating bread from God's own hand.
Fleeing from their long oppression, Israel left the past behind
And discovered in the desert boundless grace of God's design.

Forty days was Jesus tempted in a wilderness unknown,
Offered glory, fame, and honor, challenged to make bread from stone.
Hungry, thirsty, but still faithful, Jesus found the will to pray,
Turned his back on exaltation and embraced the harder way.

We must walk a weary pathway in the quest for liberty,
We must face the Tempter's offer—ease and wealth, tranquility.
Through the days of Lent we journey in a wasteland of our own,
Seeking God in barren places, finding we are not alone.

Ashes on our heads remind us of the struggle that we face
In our search for love and justice, longing for a resting place.
May we grow to be more faithful, may we follow Jesus' way
Till the clouds of Lent shall break forth on a bright new Easter day.

Penelope J. Stokes

The Rich Young Ruler—A Lenten Monologue
Matthew 19:16–30, Mark 10:17–31, Luke 18:18–30

In the sanctuary is a large cross, and the focus is on that or a handcrafted cross. A work of art that realistically portrays Christ on the cross could be projected. In either case, the actor creates the illusion that Christ is on the cross, and that there is a crowd in the midst of which the first part of this "conversation" takes place. Leave pauses in the appropriate places to suggest the unheard parts of the dialogue. At the end, remarks should be directed to Jesus on the cross.

What? Oh . . . Him! That's Jesus of Nazareth. I don't know. Blasphemy or some such thing. Messiah? (*Laugh*) I don't know who you've been listening to, but he's no Messiah. He's not even a decent rabbi.

I know because I talked to him a while back. (*Look around furtively*) Sought him out, actually. I was having a rough time. It was right after my father died.

No, no! The inheritance was all mine and there was no problem there. I have more money than I'll ever need.

I don't know, I suppose its natural to have . . . questions. What happens when we die? What's God's realm like? I was really struggling with what happened to my father, where he ended up. I mean, he was *basically* a good person, but you don't have the kind of business connections he did without rubbing elbows with a few unclean people. And I suppose he wasn't as . . . giving as he could have been to the poor *(pause)* or to me. I had heard that this Jesus of Nazareth had taught with wisdom and authority. There were even rumors of healings and exorcisms connected with him, so I thought if anyone could reassure me, tell me that I really was doing a good job, it would be him. So when I had the chance, I asked him. "Good teacher," I said, "what must I do to inherit eternal life?" At first, I liked what he had to say . . . "You know the commandments: Don't lie. Don't steal. Honor your father and mother. Do this and you will live." But then I thought, any bar mitzvah candidate knows that. His answer was too simplistic, too pat. Someone with my responsibilities and station in life deserves more attention, deeper thought. And I still wasn't satisfied. I knew there had to be more and that life had to have deeper meaning than just following the commandments My father made me learn and follow the commandments and I had done it very well. So I knew that you can follow all of those rules and still feel like something is missing, so I told him so.

And he said, "You lack one thing. Go and sell all that you have, give the money to the poor, and come follow me."

Well, I mean, that's just ridiculous! What would my servants do? Do you know how many people depend on my business for their livelihoods? But you know, he has . . . had such a way with people that I almost did it. He almost had me suckered into following him. Thank God I took some time to think about it and came to my senses. After that, I knew he wasn't the Messiah.

(Venting at Jesus, with mounting emotion)

You almost had me fooled, but you really didn't know squat. *If you are who you say you are you would have known. How sad and lonely and vulnerable I was . . . How desperately I wanted some reassurance and hope . . .* How empty this life of luxury really is. Well, look where you ended up! Follow you?!! End up with nothing, not even a legacy, and not even anyone to leave it to? I'm glad I didn't follow you! Glad! You've gained nothing! Nothing at all! I've still got my . . . my life. And I've got my . . . things! And I've got my . . . righteousness! *(long pause, emotional agitation)*

(softly) And I'd trade it all to know God loves me.

David Sickelka

5

THE RAGGED BREATHING
Words for Holy Week

[JESUS] REPLIED, "TRULY (AMEN) TODAY
YOU WILL BE WITH ME IN PARADISE."

Luke 23:43

Maundy Thursday · Matthew 26, Mark 14, Luke 22

Our God, whose wise love gave us this night of remembering failure, forgive us for leaving you, for ignoring others, for not letting your love in us have its way. Cleanse us. Open us so that the love may flow freely in and out for the sake of the world, which needs forgiveness and healing. We pray with Jesus Christ, our Savior. Amen.

Kathryn J. Campbell

Good Friday

Holy One, we gather to worship you

**even as we hear the ragged breathing of the one carrying the cross,
even as we hear him stumble and fall.**

Give us strength to hear the story once again.

Do not let us turn away from this bleak day.

Be with us in this darkness.

Jane O. Sorenson

Before the I of God

beneath the "I" of God it came,
your cross cutting hallowed space;

it seemed before we could see You,
if gazing high enough we peered;

your narrow beam of telling glass,
the single pane you enter

here beneath your star-choked dome,
ourselves taken into one,

split as light yet bound the same,
stone and vine and broken wood

sliced through splintered edge of cross,
before the I of God I come.

William B. Jones

Good Friday · Psalm 91

Oh God, under whose wings all your creatures find shelter, to you we flee this night of grief. From evil within and evil around, protect us. Keep us always near the cross, which is our hope and our assurance that the power of sin and death is broken and that your reign of mercy and justice will continue forever. Amen.

Kathryn J. Campbell

A Reflection on the Seven Last Words

We have gathered, O God, in this hour, to stand at the foot of the cross.

We have gathered to remember the story once again, to relive the suffering of Jesus, to hear Your Word in the words of his dying hours, to touch and feel and learn from the compassion and wisdom that flow in the chambers of your breaking heart.

And Jesus said, "Forgive them, Father, for they know not what they do."
Luke 23:34

In the dreadful presence of death, you teach the power of forgiveness. Lead us to forgive rather than to judge, to seek the holy in every person, to heal rather than to destroy our relationships.

And Jesus said, "Today, I tell you, you will be with me in Paradise." *Luke 23:43*

In the depths of despair, You offer the hope and promise of new life. Move us to live our lives fully, offering such hope to others, building a future founded on your vision of one just and merciful Beloved Community on Earth.

And Jesus said to Mary, "Behold your son," and to John, "Behold your mother." *John 19:27*

In the throes of loss, you offer us to one another. Teach us to love one another with the love of Christ that knows no boundaries and repairs all our divisions.

And Jesus cried out, "My God, My God, why have You forsaken me?" *Matthew 27:46*

In the dark and twisted landscape of doubt and unbelief, You show us that doubt is the pathway to faith. As we wrestle with an incomplete understanding of You, with disbelief that so much Goodness can allow such evil, help us to take responsibility for meeting and undoing the evils in our own lives, and transform our doubts into insight, a dawning awareness of Your purpose.

And Jesus simply said, "I thirst." *John 19:28*

In the drowning waves of overwhelming need, You affirm the purpose of our desires. Lead us to live our lives in balance, allowing our passions to motivate us to do justice and love kindness and walk humbly with You, the One who meets our thirst with Living Water.

And Jesus sighed, "It is finished." *John 19:30*

Lost in the details of surviving each day, you remind us that life is filled with ending that must be noted. Teach us with every ending to celebrate our accomplishments, to rest and reflect on the beauty and meaning of each completed season of our lives, to cherish each breath, to affirm our mortality as a rite of passage—into eternal life in Your Divine Presence.

And Jesus said, "Father, into Your hands I commend my Spirit." *Luke 23:46*

Fearing what we do not see and cannot know, You encourage us to place our lives into your hands. Give us the courage and the vision to do as Jesus has done, shaping our lives to Your Will, finding in you our new beginning.

ALL: We have gathered to remember, to hear, to learn, to grow. May our lives be changed by the words of your Suffering Servant. May the world be transformed by the coming resurrection of your healing, redeeming Light—Jesus Christ. Amen.

Anne G. Cohen

~

TELLING THE STORY:
An Interactive Holy Week Drama and Communion Liturgy

I am the chaplain at the Allendale Association in Lake Villa, Illinois—a child mental health facility for young people ages eight to twenty-one who suffer mental illnesses and severe behavioral disorders caused by some form of psychological trauma. One of my responsibilities is to prepare and lead a weekly chapel service for thirty to forty young people and staff from the residential program.

My primary audience is not familiar with even basic Bible stories. The majority also have learning disabilities and often performed behind their grade level. Further, most have histories of severe abuse and neglect, leaving them with significant spiritual, emotional, and psychological scars.

Designing worship for this context brings to light many of the questions that most worship leaders face: How do we make worship relevant and understandable to people who come from a variety of educational backgrounds and intellectual abilities? How do we make worship interesting and exciting to young people? How do we make the Christian message understandable to people who may have never heard it before? How do we preach a gospel of love to those who are deeply wounded?

The following drama and communion liturgy attempts to bring the Gospel of Matthew alive during Holy Week. It is short, interactive, and fun—all things that I've found to engage young people. Rituals like communion are integral to my ministry. The powerful visual symbols and visceral acts of eating and drinking live out Jesus' gospel in a way that mere words cannot. For many in my congregation, this was their first exposure to the Holy Week story and to the practice of communion. I took scripture readings from Eugene Peterson's The Message.

This week is called Holy Week. This week, Christians spend time remembering Jesus' life and the things that led up to his death. We remember that Jesus *spent time* with people he wasn't supposed to—tax collectors, prostitutes, and lepers. He *did* things he wasn't supposed to—he healed the sick on the day of rest; he called young people, poor people, and women to be his disciples.

Entering Jerusalem Like a King

We remember that only a few days before his crucifixion, the people celebrated Jesus and called him "The King of the Jews." They took palm branches and waved them and yelled, "Hosanna, Hosanna in the highest!" Try that—

wave your palms and say, "Hosanna in the Highest!" We're going to read the story of Jesus entering Jerusalem from the Gospel of Matthew. And when you hear the word, "Hosanna!" wave your palms.

Reader 1 reads Matthew 21:6–11.

A Meal with Friends

We remember that after Jesus entered Jerusalem, he spent a few days preaching and teaching. He told stories in order to teach people about God. And some of the things Jesus said upset the people in charge. Jesus was too kind to the people who had no power. He believed in helping them, even if that meant bending the rules a little bit.

But one rule that he followed in that time was observing the Passover. The Passover was a time when Jews (of which Jesus was one) remembered that they had been liberated from slavery in Egypt and that the angel of death had passed over their homes.

Reader 2 reads Matthew 26:17–19

And Jesus celebrated the Passover with his friends, even though he knew one of his friends had turned him in to the authorities for a little bit of money. He worshiped with his friends, even though he knew they would all abandon him after he was arrested and put to death. He worshiped with them even though one of them would deny that he even knew Jesus.

Killed like a Criminal

Jesus was arrested later that night. His friends abandoned him and the Roman authorities were trying to figure out what to do with him. Pilate, the governor of Jerusalem, offered the crowd a choice—they could release a well-known murderer named Barabbas or Jesus.

Reader 31 reads Matthew 27:21–23

So they released Barabbas and took Jesus along with two other criminals to be killed. They beat Jesus, put a crown of thorns on his head, nailed him to a cross and made fun of him. For three hours in the hot afternoon sun, Jesus hung on the cross. When he was about to die, he said, "My God, my God, why have you abandoned me?" And then he died.

Coming to the Table

Tonight we are going to celebrate communion. We remember the Passover meal that Jesus shared with his friends—the friends who betrayed and abandoned him and the friends who later risked their own lives to tell Jesus' story.

We remember that we too have betrayed Jesus. We remember that at other times we have followed Jesus, even if we suffer because of it. Now, I want to ask each of us to take a moment to silently confess our sins and ask God to forgive them.

Silence

God, like people in Jesus' time, we both sing your praises and betray you every day. By eating this special meal today, help us to let go of the past and take hold of the future that you are planning for us. We pray this in the name of Jesus, the liberator. Amen.

We remember that at that Passover meal he shared with his friends, Jesus took the bread, broke it, gave thanks to God and said, "This is my body, broken for you so that all people may know God's love. Do this in memory of me." Then, Jesus took the cup, poured it out, gave thanks to God and said, "This is the cup of my blood, the cup of God's new promise to save everyone from sin. Do this in memory of me."

God, pour out your spirit upon our gifts of bread and juice. Bless them with the power of your Son, who chose death so that we may all know life. In his name we pray. Amen.

Distribute Communion Elements

Thanksgiving

God, we thank you for the gift of life you have given us through this meal. Help us to remember your Son's sacrifice, which made our own lives possible. In his name, we pray. Amen.

Nicole M. Havelka

VOICES IN JERUSALEM:
Worship for Palm-Passion Sunday (or any day in Holy Week)

The Hebrew word, "kol" means "voice." It refers to the outer voices we hear with our ears, but also to God's voice, which we hear with our hearts. This worship drama is based on the Gospel of Mark. We will hear scripture, as well as "listen in" on some of the participants in those events. The shofar is an ancient musical instrument, used by the Jewish faith even to this day. The voice of the shofar in today's worship connects us with God's ancient but timeless work for redemption.

Opening Prayer (Unison)

Transport us to Jerusalem today, O Spirit, that we may spend some time with Jesus. Help us to hear his teaching, feel his healing, and follow his example. Let us meet Jesus in our hearts that we may take Christ into our world today. Now we open our lives so that you may take us where we need to go, making Jesus Christ real for us not only in Passion but in the Compassion of God's Love for all. Amen.

A moment of silence to calm our heads and open our hearts. The shofar sounds a tekiah *(a long, unbroken blast), a wake-up call to our spirits, calling us into worship.*

Procession with Palms

The Story from Scripture · Mark 11:1–10

VOICE 1: I am one of Jesus' disciples. And I have a question. Why did Jesus want a little colt? The Messiah ought to come to the throne on a mighty war horse! Didn't he know how ridiculous he looked on the back of that donkey?

VOICE 2: What a great day! I haven't had this much fun in ages! Did you see that rabbi Jesus enter the city? He came in like a crazy little king. Pilate comes charging in on his chariot, leading his army. Jesus trotted in followed by a bunch of peasants. We all grabbed branches and waved them high, shouting and cheering. What a great day!

VOICE 3: I waved a branch today, too. And I laughed. But even more, I hoped. I hoped that maybe this Jesus means to change things. I'm just like one of those peasants following him. They know how hard life is. Jesus knows, too. So hoping that just maybe he might be a new messiah, I joined the crowds that shouted:

CROWD: *(shouting)* Hosanna! Hosanna in the highest! Hosanna! Hosanna!

The shofar sounds a shevarim *(three shorter blasts), reminding us of the brokenness of life, and a large metal bowl or platter is placed on the altar. Coins are poured into it noisily.*

VOICE 4: That Jesus is nothing but trouble! He came into the city today and went straight to the Temple. He started yelling and pushed over the tables where the coins were exchanged and sacrificial doves were sold. He scared people away by saying we had made the temple into a den of robbers! He said it should be a house of prayer for all nations. All nations! Are we supposed to let just *anybody* in?

VOICE 1: That Jesus is trouble! He goes around forgiving sins and healing and teaching that everyone can know God. No one made him a priest. Nobody gave him permission. Who gave him any authority to do these things?

VOICE 2: That Jesus is real trouble! We tried to catch him saying something wrong. We asked him if it was legal to pay taxes to Rome. Instead of taking the bait, he asked whose image was on the coin. When we took one out and showed him that Caesar's image was on it, he looked at us as if to say that it was clear where our true allegiance lay. Then all he said was to give to Caesar what belonged to Caesar, but to give to God what is God's. He made us look like fools and sell-outs. Jesus is *serious* trouble!

The Story from Scripture · Mark 11:15–18

A large scroll is placed on the altar.

VOICE 3: That Jesus is amazing! I am a scribe, so I know the Law. I asked Jesus which commandment is first of all. Even the elders have debated this. But Jesus spoke right up and said: "The first is, 'Hear, O Israel: the Lord our God, the Lord is one; you shall love the Lord your God with all your heart, and with all your soul, and with all your mind, and with all your strength.' The second is this, 'You shall love your neighbor as yourself.' There is no other commandment greater than these."

VOICE 4: That Jesus is amazing! For years I've felt invisible. I am poor and a widow, but I serve God as best I can. I gave my last two pennies, knowing that two cents won't keep me in food or shelter. I gave them because God will have to keep me now. But Jesus saw me bring my offering to God. He said my gift was greater than all those others. That Jesus is amazing, he was the only one who saw me!

The Story from Scripture · Mark 12:41–44

Plates of bread and a pitcher of wine are brought forward to the table.

Voice 1: So much of what Jesus did, he did around the supper table. He even welcomed us women to eat with him. Women have always had to wait to eat until the men are done! But Jesus wanted us all there together, as equals. I could see that while Jesus claimed us all as friends, he was making real enemies in Jerusalem. I was afraid that no one was taking this danger seriously. So at dinner one night, I came in and anointed Jesus for his burial. Some of the men were outraged. Jesus said I would be remembered for my vision.

Voice 2: So much of what Jesus did, he did around the supper table. We were celebrating Passover together, all of us. Passover reminds us how God set us free from bondage in Egypt. Jesus said the unleavened bread was his body. The cup left for Elijah, the symbol of our hope for God to act, Jesus said that was his blood. It is to be a new covenant for everybody.

Voice 3: Jesus meant *everybody*. He said one of us would betray him, and he told Peter that he would deny him, and that we would all run away. And still, Jesus shared the meal, and the covenant with us all. What Jesus did at the supper table was to claim every last one of us as his family, no matter what.

The Story from Scripture · Mark 14:22–25

While they were eating, Jesus took a loaf of bread, and after blessing it he broke it, gave it to them, and said, "Take; this is my body." Then he took a cup, and after giving thanks he gave it to them, and all of them drank from it. He said to them, "This is my blood of the covenant, which is poured out for many. Truly I tell you, I will never again drink of the fruit of the vine until that day when I drink it new in the realm of God."

Communion Prayer (Unison)

Let us pray.

God of justice and compassion, in remembrance of these your mighty acts in Jesus Christ, we offer ourselves in praise and thanksgiving as a holy and living sacrifice, in union with Christ's offering for us. Pour out your Holy Spirit on us, and on these gifts of bread and wine. Make them be for us the body and blood of Christ, that we may be for the world the body of Christ, redeemed by Christ's blood. By your Spirit make us one with Christ, one with each other, and one in ministry to all the world until Christ comes with peace, and all your children may feast united together. Amen.

Communion is shared and the shofar sounds the teruah *(ten short, staccato blasts), a groaning and yearning for God's restoration of the world. A black cloth is draped on the altar.*

The Story from Scripture · Mark 14:32–38

VOICE 4: I was one of those Jesus invited to pray with him. But there was a gentle breeze that night, and we had eaten so much. I knew he was troubled. I wanted to be there for him. I watched him as he prayed. He cried. I fell asleep. Why couldn't I stay wake with him?

VOICE 1: I am Judas, and I know what you think of me. Don't ask me why I did what I did. I'm not sure that I even know. What seemed so clear in the day became confused in the night. I led the thugs and guards to the garden where they could capture Jesus. I stayed at a distance and watched for a long time. I think I hoped they would hear us come as Jesus was praying and be able to escape. But they all fell asleep, all except Jesus, and he was wrapped up in prayer. Finally the guards compelled me to act. I knew it was all coming apart. Jesus didn't flinch. I kissed him for all he had meant to me. I kissed him to beg forgiveness. I kissed him, the guards grabbed him, and every one of his disciples deserted him.

CROWD: *(shouting)* We are the guards who have come to seize Jesus. We brought swords and clubs, even though he taught peace. Grab him now!

VOICE 2: I have heard blasphemy and torn my robe. I am the high priest who questioned Jesus. We knew he was trouble from the moment he showed up in Jerusalem. He just got bolder and bolder. When I asked him if he was the Messiah, he said he was! Rome is nervous enough at festival time; at least we can quiet this rabble-rouser.

VOICE 3: I can't believe what I did! I can't believe the words that came pouring out of my mouth! They grabbed him and questioned him and condemned him right there. They spit on him and taunted him as I watched. *I denied I ever knew him!* Not once but three times . . .

The Story from Scripture · Mark 14:66–72

The sound of a rooster crowing twice is heard, and during a hymn a chain is brought in and placed on or in front of the altar.

The Story in Scripture · Mark 15:6-20

VOICE 4: I am Pilate, Roman governor of Jerusalem and Palestine. I hate the festivals when hordes of peasants come pouring into the city. You just know someone will bring up this "messiah" myth and start talking rebellion. This Jesus was a sorry example. How anyone would think he could be a king is beyond me. He didn't even seem to be a militant or a rebel. Too much noise and too much trouble. That is what got Jesus killed. Rome does not tolerate insurrection of any kind. Jesus became the example of Rome's complete power over these peasants.

CROWD: *(shouting)* Earlier this week we waved our palm branches and shouted "Hosanna!" Now we call, "Crucify! Crucify! Crucify!"

VOICE 1: We made ourselves a king today! I'm one of Pilate's soldiers and he gave us the "King of Jews" to crucify. So we found an old purple blanket and made it his robe. We made a crown of thorns and had a royal coronation. We pledged our loyalty and never laughed so hard. Then we got to work.

A purple cloth is placed around the cross on the altar. A crown of thorns may also be placed there. After a hymn, a drum begins beating slowly. It increases in intensity throughout this section, culminating at the end of the scripture reading.

VOICE 2: I have never felt a cross before. I'm the Simon they forced to carry the cross-beam Jesus dropped. He was so weak. It cut my hands and left splinters under my skin. I was afraid that when we got to Skull Hill they would nail me right up there with him. I ran away as soon as they let me go, the pounding ringing in my ears.

CROWD: *(shouting)* Jesus, you said you would destroy the Temple and rebuild it in three days! Messiah! King of Israel! See how you have been lifted up!

VOICE 3: I don't know how Jesus had breath left enough to cry out like that. All his followers ran away like sheep. Not one came to stand with him. As a Roman soldier, I've seen men cry on the cross before. But he cried that even God had forgotten him. It's enough to make you believe in something greater than yourself.

The Story in Scripture · Mark 15:21–24

Silence. Christ has died.

Prayer of Confession (Unison)

Too often we leave you on the cross, O Jesus. We have heard you teach and felt your healing touch. But somehow we prefer you hanging silent. Open our hearts to reach out wherever people suffer that we may minister to you. You faced the forces of violence with peace and love and conquered them by compassion. Open our hearts to feel the love of God, who desires peace above blood. Forgive us our ability to be bystanders when Christ needs us to act in love. Too often we leave you on the cross, O Jesus. Forgive us still. Amen.

Offertory and the Prayer of Our Savior

A white linen cloth is draped on the altar.

The Story in Scripture · Mark 15:42–47

Voice 4: I am Mary, the one you probably do not know. I watched it all happen. I saw the others run away. I saw Jesus crucified. I watched him cry out and breathe his last. I saw Joseph take his body. I know the tomb where they have laid his body. The Sabbath is starting, so we can't touch the body now. But I will watch the tomb until Sabbath is over and then I will finish the burial rituals. Jesus deserves that last act of compassion. Will you watch with me until Sabbath is over?

The shofar sounds the tekiah gedolah *(a single blast, held as long as possible), calling us to repentance and signaling the end of our worship.*

Doyle Burbank Williams

6

A NEW DAY HAS BEGUN

Words for Easter

Now may the God of peace, who brought back from the dead our Lord Jesus, the great shepherd of the sheep, by the blood of the eternal covenant, make you complete in everything good so that you may do his will, working among us that which is pleasing in his sight, through Jesus Christ, to whom be the glory forever and ever. Amen

Hebrews 13:20

Call to Worship

The community has gathered.

We have come to hear the good news.

Hear the good news: Jesus Christ has risen!

We have come to worship the risen Christ!

Now is the time for worship.

We will worship now!

Hallelujah! Let us worship together!

Susan E. Brown

Easter

Gracious and loving God, who took the horror of what we did to your Child and turned it into new life: hear our prayer this morning. We have chosen the world's cares over your Child's easy yoke. We have looked for smooth paths, when your Child would have led us over difficult ones. We have hidden our faces from you. Holy One, remind us: You who raise Jesus from the dead can raise us to new life. Bring healing to our broken places, bring your peace to our anger and our fear, and bring your tender mercy to us, that we might know ourselves forgiven and ready to begin again.

Jane O. Sorenson

Call to Worship

Look! The dawn is breaking. Morning is on its way. See, on the hillside the sun is beginning to rise!

Leave us alone and let us sleep. We want to forget about the terrors of the night. We want to shut out the darkness.

Look! The tomb is open. A new day has begun.

Leave us alone and let us grieve. We have lost our hope, and all our dreams are dead.

But look! The grave is empty. The stone is rolled away.

An empty grave? A vacant shroud? Then hope is reborn, and the dream is alive again. Death has been swallowed up in victory. Rejoice, for the day of resurrection has come at last. Alleluia!

Prayer of Confession

God of new awakenings, we confess that we would rather stay asleep. We are afraid to hope and have our hopes shattered. We are afraid to dream and find our dreams deferred. Break us open like the tomb so that new life may pour forth. Give us the faith to believe, to hope, to dream anew. Let us live as people of your resurrection. Amen.

Words of Assurance

Christ has risen from the grave to bring us out of the shadow of death, to free us from all fear, to liberate our souls into newness of life. This is good news indeed. Thanks be to God.

Offertory Sentence

Christ conquers death and leads us into the path of life. Let us live graciously and give generously, as God has given generously to us.

Offertory Dedication

The gift of resurrection reminds us that all we possess comes to us by the grace of God. May these gifts and offerings serve as a token of our love and gratefulness. May they be used to further God's justice and love in the world. May we live in new life, and share that life with others. Amen.

Unison Prayer

God of endings and new beginnings, we come to worship and to praise. We come to abandon our pretenses and offer up our hope and dreams, that you may breathe new life into them. Shake us from our slumber and awaken us to our own resurrections. Open our eyes to the new day dawning in our hearts. Let us rejoice and be glad, for life has triumphed over death! Alleluia! Amen.

Penelope J. Stokes

Day One

wondering what next after this,
he woke to cave's pierced-darkness
edged by light stone sought to block,
but could not this bright morning

loosing the wrappings death held close,
falling to floor he reaches his hand
un-bent, un-bleeding, into cool air
and, risking life, begins breathing

slowly it dawns it has been undone,
bruised yet healing from wounding
wondering what next after this,
he rises and eases through walls

clinging close the still-moist earth,
upending the plot tended by mourners
stumbling, tripping what they hadn't sought,
newly un-dead, rooting deep seed

pulling himself up into the living,
harder than dying his hand gripping mine
dried blood and cooling the fever his brow,
he rises and eases through walls.

William B. Jones

Hymn—The Women Came at Early Dawn (tune—"St. Anne")
Mark 16:1–8; Matthew 26:1–10; Luke 24:1–12)

The women came at early dawn to visit Jesus' tomb.
They came discouraged and forlorn. Their hearts were filled with gloom.

As they approached, they wondered who would roll away the stone.
But soon they found it strange but true, they were not there alone.

A messenger spoke loud and clear and told them what took place.
The herald told them not to fear; it was an act of grace.

"He is not here; come, see the place; He's risen from the dead.
He's now alive; you'll see his face. It's happened as he said.

"So now go forth to Galilee to meet the risen One,
by death once held but now set free. A new age has begun."

The Easter song is ours to sing to share our joy today.
And now we'll keep on traveling along the pilgrim way.

Robert A. Lewis

7

ANOINTING INTO THE WORLD
Words for Eastertide

For in [Jesus Christ] every one
of God's promises is a "Yes." For this
reason it is through him that we say
the "Amen," to the glory of God.

2 Corinthians 1: 20

Unison Prayer

Risen Savior,
In love, you came to earth as the Anointed One
    to set apart, prepare, and send out your faithful.
In love, this community finds its purpose
    in serving those whom you have anointed.
In love, we carry our anointing into the world
    so that we might fulfill the call
you have placed in each of our lives.
In the name of the One
who has formed, redeemed,
and inspired this community, Amen.

Susan E. Brown

Call to Worship

Unlock your hearts—God wants to come in.

Open your lives—God needs a home.

Swing wide all the doors—God's children need shelter.

Easter rolls the stone—

> **and nothing can be shut anymore!**

Maren C. Tirabassi

Holy One,
You who give me life,
I come to you as a child,
holding your hand,
walking through days and nights,
through seasons of joy and sadness,
busyness and quiet,
crowds and solitude.
I am held in the hands
once crucified,
healed in the loving arms
embracing me
in eternal love that whispers,
"You are my child,
in whom I am well pleased."
Blessed be. Amen.

Sue Henley

Call to Worship · Psalm 150

God's being-and-doing extends far beyond greatness.

Praise God in the sanctuary!

God astounds us in the words and music we come to share this morning.

Praise God with tambourine and dance, strings and cymbals!

In our inhales and exhales, in our gathering and in our releasing, in our pondering and in our praying, we praise!

Alleluia! Praise God!

Prayer of Invocation

In the wake of the Rising of the One we call Christ, we gather as a people of sanctuary, as a people of Sabbath, ever seeking God's presence, ever in awe of the new life around us. Accept our music as gift, our words as offering, our dance as service, our breath as worship. Amen.

Confession · John 20:19–31

O God, I confess my doubt to you, for it is deep and wide, like a fresh wound whose sting cannot be softened by any ointment or bandage. One moment, I praise with song and dance, and the next moment, I turn away from you. I mistakenly beg for certainty, proof, and control over that which cannot be known or controlled. I cry out, "Show me!" My doubt suffocates me even while you breathe on and within me. Open space for me enough to breathe in the reality of your presence in all that I do, in all that I seek, in all that I doubt, and restore new life in me that I may know belief in you, which is deeper and wider than any doubt. Guide my questions that they may expand my awareness and trust amidst the unknown, the mystery, the inexplicable.

Assurance · Revelation 1:4–8

God loves us and frees us from all that we do to turn away from the transformative power of belief. God hears our cries and questions. God promises to remain in covenant. In the name of the Rising One, who came, who comes, and who is to come again, the heavy weight of doubt is lifted.

Call to Offering

To praise God is to both give and receive. In this moment, we meditate on both as we prepare to give as we are able in the sanctuary of spirit and service. In gratitude for that which we receive from God who works upon, within, and between each of us in this gathered body, we open our hearts and our hands.

Dedication

Let us pray. God, bless these gifts that they may be shared in the spirit of an Easter people, ever seeking ways to live out faith in acts of service. Amen.

Elizabeth D. Barnum

Another Look at Psalm 150: Call to worship

Praise God with piano and percussion,
with flute and kazoo,
with descant and download.

Praise God with iPod and live journal;
praise God with "my space" become "God's space."

Praise the I AM with Instant Messenger,
the One who is in every cell of the universe—with cell phone.

Praise God with the tambourine of traffic,
the tympani of lift-off at airport,
trumpet of motorcycle, autoharp of skateboard.

Praise God with the dance of television—
the chorus line of reality shows, tap-dance of news,
ballet of the weather channel,
two-step of sitcom, Macarena of "Makeover."

Praise God with dish and DVD, bells and blog,
with text and text message, voice mail and e-mail.

Praise God with surprising music—
the google of teen and the giggle of child.

Let every music, every message,
every muscle, every minute praise God.
Let everything that has breath—Praise God!

Maren C. Tirabassi

A Ploem* on Life

In the beginning was *Spirit* . . .
and it was good and abundant and powerful and playful and full of itself . . .

So it splashed and splattered here and there
and dripped and dropped everywhere,
Sharing its lushness and wetness and generosity . . .

And wherever it splashed and splattered, dripped and dropped
it completed itself
And a wideness was added to its wetness . . .

Until one day it felt stronger and bigger. . .
and its wideness welcomed its firmness
And it began to walk and stop and run . . .

Then its firmness welcomed its wonder and it walked to and fro,
up and down, over and under and all around itself . . .
until it could chase itself all over the place.

Soon it noticed that its place had shifted so much . . .
there was no place it could not be, without *Being*!

And its *Being* was good and abundant and powerful and playful and full of itself!

And it began to notice that its *Beingness* took on new shapes and sizes and
colors and sounds until before long it became a *Rainbow of Being* . . .

Spirit saw it was beautiful . . . and it began to understand that its
Becoming was full of surprises . . . and a giggle was born.

At first it was soft and silent but as it began to discover its wetness
and wideness and firmness and difference and beauty . . .

The giggle grew and grew . . . until one day *Laughter* burst forth from its silence
and there was *Dancing*!

Joy and wonder leaped into the air and water and air joined hands,
and *Spirit* liked being firm and free and grounded all at the same time.

When it discovered its firmness and freeness was inside and outside too . . .
Spirit laughed itself silly . . . just for the fun of it.

Then sleep came and *Spirit* rested on its firmness . . . and it was night.

In the blink of an eye, the first day came to a close . . .
except that on the other side of *Spirit's* wideness, light was dawning
and life was stirring and yawning and stretching . . . and . . .

Well . . . I could tell you more . . . but I need to close my eyes because . . .
Tomorrow is another day . . .

And when *Tomorrow* comes calling . . . I want to be ready for anything!

**A "Ploem is an unfinished poem that is meant to be played with . . .
over and over, so that whenever it is shared, Spirit has its way.*

June Goudey

Call to Worship · Psalm 30

Rising One, come to me this day. Transform dark to light.

Returning One, come to me this day. Hear and then soften the sounds of my cries.

Rising One, come to me this day. Wake me and move me to dance.

Returning One, come to me this day. Sing in me songs of peace.

Rising One, come to me this day. Appear over and over again.

Returning One, turn toward us as we turn toward you during this season of Easter.

Elizabeth D. Barnum

23 reprise

if I into grace yet stumble,
if in silence come to peace,

if I echo rod and staff,
if in death I find release

if I valley into life,
if I out into amen

if I fool for Jesus promise,
if I crush You please redeem.

William B. Jones

Collect for Eastertide

Holy God,
our good shepherd,
lead us to the peace and calmness
that restore our souls;
so that we may live faithfully
in Jesus Christ our Savior.

Patricia Catellier

RESOURCES FOR EASTERTIDE

Commissioning for Easter

ONE: When you find yourself lost and confused,

Two: may you hear Christ calling your name.

ONE: As you venture on uncertain pathways,

Two: may you recognize Christ with you on the journey.

ONE: In times of wondering and doubt,

Two: may you feel Christ's patient reassurance.

ONE: And in all times and places know this:

ONE and two together: Christ is risen!

ALL: Alleluia! Amen.

Confession · John 20:19–23

God of resurrection power,
break through the locked doors of our certainty
to encourage our wonderings and our questions.
Break through the walls of our fears of others,
that we might make room for all at your table
Break through our doubt and confusion,
that we might come to know your presence
more fully in our lives and in our world.
When we seek to judge ourselves and others
for disbelief and questions,
open the locked doors of our hearts
and give us the patience of the risen Christ,
in whose name we pray. Amen.

Assurance

As Christ broke into the disciples' locked room, offering forgiveness and the breath of new life, so Christ can enter our closed hearts and minds and give us new life. Know that you are forgiven. Feel the breath of resurrection creating you anew.

ALL: Thanks be to God. Amen.

Call to Worship or Commissioning

Christ is risen!

Stones of fear are rolled away.

Christ is risen!

Walls of prejudice are broken down.

Christ is risen!

Doubts are affirmed; questions are allowed.

Christ is risen!

Those who were pushed aside are welcomed in.

Christ is risen!

Life will never be the same again.

Christ is risen! Alleluia!

(option 1) Come, let us worship God.

(option 2) Go in peace, to proclaim the good news.

Invocation · Acts 16:11–15

Paul had a vision in the night: "Come to Macedonia and help us."

Open us to your call to go to new places, O God.

Paul talked theology with the women at the river.

Open us to share faith with those we meet, whoever and wherever they are.

Lydia listened to the good news Paul brought.

Open us to hear the new message of Christ's love and justice.

Lydia convinced Paul to stay at her home.

Open us to change our plans for the sake of the gospel. Amen.

Donald Schmidt

Call to Worship—Fifth Sunday in Eastertide

I am too busy; I cannot praise my God.

My time hangs too heavily on my hands; I cannot praise my God.

There is too much wrong in the world; I cannot praise my God.

There is too much noise in the world; I cannot praise my God.

There is too much quiet in my world; I cannot praise my God.

There are reasons beyond count to explain why I cannot praise my God.

I am lonely, I am tired, I am overworked, I have no resources for such a task.

Take our sore places and comfort us.

Take our weary places and give us rest.

Take our reasons and overwrite them with your love for us

    and your need for us to be the people you created us to be. Amen.

Jane O. Sorenson

Confession for Ascension Sunday · Psalm 93, Ephesians 1:15–23

God of heights, lift us up:

    We are crawling in the mire of everyday routine.

God of the heavens, lift us up:

    We are overwhelmed with the attention required by the things of this earth.

God of the stars, lift us up:

    We cannot see past the clouds of "truth" that some would have us believe.

God of the sun, lift us up:

    We are dazzled by the false jewels of society.

God of the moon, lift us up:

    We are taxed by others' demands for us to shine for them.

God of the universe, lift us up:

    We want to stretch and breathe and see and be awe-struck.

God of heights, lift us up.

Rachel G. Hackenberg

Jailhouse Flock *(tune—Elvis' famous hit "Jailhouse Rock")* · Acts 16:16–34

Paul and Silas threw a party in the county jail.

The prison band was there and they began to wail.

A big earthquake came and the joint began to shake.

You should've seen those freaked-out jailbirds quake.

Chorus: Let's rock, everybody, let's rock.

Everybody in the whole cell block

Was dancin' with the jailhouse flock.

The doors flew open, it was their chance to vamoose,

People's chains came free, they were loose as a goose,

The guard's feelin' blue, "Whatever will I do?

I'll be fired, thrown out, sent packing, man, I'm through!"

Shifty Henry said to Paul, For heaven's sake,
no one's lookin, now's our chance to make a break.
Paul turned to Shifty and said, No way,
I wanna stay here and make the prison guard's day.

The sad sack was sittin' on a block of stone
way over in the corner weepin' all alone.
So ol' Paul said, What you *got* to do,
Is believe in the Lord, man, and you'll be saved too.

So the guard took Paul and Silas home with him,
Everybody there joined him in baptism.
The guard washed their wounds, & fed them a good meal,
They were jumpin' for joy, 'cuz God was so real.

Chorus: **Let's rock, everybody, let's rock.**
Everybody in the whole cell block
Was dancin' with the jailhouse flock.

Tom Nalesnik

TESTIFY TO LOVE: A Story for All Ages Series

Sundays after Easter everyone expects low attendance from the congregation and low energy from the pastor. This series reminds everyone that resurrection is never over. Consider inviting your congregation to share in the practice of testimony each week, or during a special service the week following the three weeks these skits are used.

Episode One · John 20:19–31

Cast: Bailiff—Small part for someone willing to have some fun but not a big public speaker. Lawyer—A "just the facts" kind of person who eventually discovers that there is more to life than simply what can be quantified. Thomas— Not such a doubter anymore.

BAILIFF: All rise! Court is now in session. Please place your hand on the Bible. Do you swear to tell the truth, the whole truth, and nothing but the truth, so help you God?

THOMAS: I do.

LAWYER: Okay, Thomas. There are a lot of us around here who are wondering how exactly we can be sure that Jesus rose from the dead. You've got a reputation for being a clear-thinking man, so we'd like you to tell us exactly what you saw. Just the facts, please.

THOMAS: Well, I saw Jesus die on the cross and I am 100 percent certain that he was dead by the end of the day. I saw the tomb where they laid his body. There was a huge stone blocking the entrance to the tomb and guards stationed there. No one was going to be sneaking over there and taking his body out.

LAWYER: Excellent. Now go on about the resurrection.

THOMAS: Well, it happened a few days later. But I didn't actually see it with my own eyes.

LAWYER: What?! Then how can you be so sure it happened?

THOMAS: Actually, that was my attitude too. My friends were out of their minds with excitement about what they'd seen, but I wasn't going to be taken for a ride. I told them I wouldn't believe Jesus had risen from the dead until I saw him with my own eyes, and what's more, until I touched his wounds with my own hands.

LAWYER (to congregation): Ah, a man after my own heart! (to Thomas) So, that's what you did, right? You held out until you had direct physical evidence?

THOMAS: Well yes . . . but then again, no . . . I mean, sort of.

LAWYER: Speak up, man! Did you or did you not touch the resurrected body of Jesus?

THOMAS: Uh, I forget . . .

LAWYER: *You forget???* Have you lost your mind???

THOMAS: No, I haven't lost my mind, but my thinking has changed. Let me explain: A week later, Jesus did come and show himself to us again. We were all together in a room, the door was locked, and yet suddenly we could see him standing there among us. He spoke directly to me! He held out his hands and offered to let me touch them.

LAWYER: And you did, right?

THOMAS: No, I actually fell on the floor.

LAWYER: *Jesus tripped you??*

THOMAS: No, I was just overcome with awe, I . . . I . . . I . . . can't explain it. When I saw him there, I forgot all about my questions and my doubts. My heart was on fire. I felt like it wasn't just him who was resurrected—I felt like it was me, too! I was born that day . . . I became a new man . . .

LAWYER: Please! Get a hold of yourself! I need you to focus here. Now you say the door was locked. Who had the key besides you? Were you on the first floor? Were there any open windows in the room where someone could gain access? And what exactly did Jesus look like? Was he solid, or was he kind of see-through . . .

THOMAS *(interrupting)*: You don't get it, do you? That's not the kind of evidence you really need. Jesus is alive—not just in that room, not just to his disciples. He's alive in our hearts, and he's afoot in the world. God's resurrecting power is everywhere! I don't know how it happened but all I can say is I'm changed because of his love!

Episode Two · Luke 24:36b–48

Cast: Bailiff, Lawyer, Disciple 1, Disciple 2—Disciples who just recently returned from Emmaus.

BAILIFF: All rise! Court is now in session. Please place your hand on the Bible. Do you swear to tell the truth, the whole truth, and nothing but the truth, so help you God?

DISCIPLES: I do.

LAWYER: Okay, we are here to uncover the truth of what happened on Easter. In your own words can you tell us what happened?

DISCIPLE 1: Well, you see we first met Jesus on the road to Emmaus.

DISCIPLE 2: Only we didn't know it was Jesus until he broke the bread.

LAWYER: Didn't know it was Jesus? You were his disciples. How could you not have known it was him? This sounds highly suspect. And what does bread have to do with it?

DISCIPLE 2: Well, we did know it was Jesus. Only not right away 'cause he had been crucified and had died. We thought that was the end of the story. We couldn't really believe he was resurrected, but then he broke bread and blessed it and gave it right to us and we knew who it was. It just took us some time to figure out but it was the bread that clinched it. Does that make sense?

LAWYER: *(making a "he's crazy" gesture and addressing the audience)* It sounds like the butter has slipped off his bread, if you know what I mean! *(Addressing the disciples)* No, it makes no sense. But go on.

DISCIPLE 1: We did recognize him, but then he vanished. We were stunned that Jesus had been with us and our hearts were going, like, a hundred miles an hour.

DISCIPLE 2: Major heart action going on there. Thump, thump, thump, thump!

DISCIPLE 1: So we rushed off to tell the others. We high-tailed it back to Jerusalem to let them know what we had seen.

DISCIPLE 2: Right. And while we were there with them Jesus came back again.

LAWYER: Wait a minute. You just told this court that he was in Emmaus and now you are telling us he was in Jerusalem too.

DISCIPLE 1: He's everywhere, don't you see? You can't pin him down. His love and power is too great for that.

LAWYER: Look, let's get back to the facts here. So he appeared to you and to your friends in Jerusalem. What did he say exactly?

DISCIPLE 2: He said, "Peace be with you." Man, you should feel the kind of peace that he gives to be in his presence. It is transforming, I mean . . .

LAWYER: Your Honor, please strike that from the record. The witness is speculating. We have no evidence for this peace.

DISCIPLE 1: But I felt it too. It is real even if you can't measure it. Then, the next thing Jesus did was have us touch him and see him so that we knew he was real. And his hands and his feet still bore the scars of crucifixion, but the pain was gone.

DISCIPLE 2: He even ate a piece of fish in our presence. Imagine—alive then dead then risen then hungry. That's Jesus for you.

LAWYER: You Honor, we are floundering here! The story gets fishier and fishier. They're trying to lure me into this tale. Can't we just stick the facts?!

DISCIPLE 1: He did tell us the most important facts there are: that God is alive and at work in the world, that redemption has been God's work all along— it's all over the Hebrew Scriptures in the Law of Moses and in the prophets and the psalms—and that it all comes together in Jesus Christ. He told us that repentance and forgiveness of sins are to be proclaimed in his name to all the nations. You have to understand, that's what we are trying to do.

LAWYER: But don't you understand that all of this is hearsay? We have no hard empirical proof. Did he say anything else?

DISCIPLE 1: One last thing. He said, "You are witnesses to these things." That's our job, to be witnesses to what God has done through Jesus Christ.

He's given us a task. He's given our lives meaning. We've got to testify. That's what we're doing.

LAWYER: You'd think that Jesus couldn't have gotten better witnesses than you two. So far you have given this court no solid evidence that we can go on. How exactly do you explain this crazy story?

BOTH DISCIPLES: We don't know how it happened, but all we can say is, we're changed!

Episode Three · John 10:11–18

Cast: Bailiff, Lawyer, Sheep

BAILIFF: All rise! Court is now in session. Please place your hand on the Bible. Do you swear to tell the truth, the whole truth, and nothing but the truth, so help you God.

SHEEP: Baaaaaaa.

LAWYER: Do we have a translator? I don't speak sheep. I thought this was an English only court room. These sheep are always asking for special privileges.

SHEEP: Oh, I'm baaaaaalingual.

LAWYER: Why didn't you say so? Okay, let's get on with this.

BAILIFF: Do you swear to tell the truth, the whole truth, and nothing but the truth, so help you God?

SHEEP: I do. I wooley do!

LAWYER: Do you know why you have been called to the witness stand, Sheep?

SHEEP: It has to do with the Good Shepherd, right? I'm part of his flock. He knows me and I know him. What more do you need to know?

LAWYER: But how exactly do you know him? That is what we are trying to get to the bottom of here.

SHEEP: Well, I know him because I belong to him. I listen to his voice and follow him.

LAWYER: You say you listen to his voice but what does that voice sound like? Can you play for this court a recording of his voice? Have you captured it on video? Can I play it on my iPod?

SHEEP: It isn't like that. I hear him, yes, but I can't play it back for you.

LAWYER: Well, when you are hearing these voices, how do you know that it's really Jesus?

SHEEP: Well, I have a personal relationship with him. If you don't believe me, ask any of the other flocks.

LAWYER: How many flocks are we talking about here?

SHEEP: More than I can count. What, you want me to start counting sheep right here in this court room?!

LAWYER: How frustrating! What did they teach me in law school—never share a courtroom with children or cute animals, and look at me now!

Okay, let's get back to the issues at hand. How can one shepherd be responsible for that many flocks? You're suggesting that this man, Jesus, is responsible for the whole world. That's absurd! I suggest, Your Honor, that the witness is referring to a lot of different shepherds. After all, one shepherd cannot be responsible for so many sheep.

SHEEP: Well he is. There is one flock and one shepherd. I'm not spinning a yarn here.

LAWYER: Hmmm. We'll leave that one for a moment and move on. Sheep, why is it that you follow him? How do you know he is for real?

SHEEP: Well, that is simple. I follow him because I love him. I belong to him.

LAWYER: Well, be that as it may, I see you standing here today and I don't see Jesus with you. If you belong to him, where is he? Has he abandoned you while you are trying to testify about him?

SHEEP: No, quite the opposite. He's right here in my heart. He loves me so much that he lays down his life for me. You know, you've probably heard about hired hands, right? Well, they're not exactly bad, but when a wolf shows up they run for it. But the Good Shepherd isn't afraid to be with us when things are really hard. In fact, when I feel most in danger or alone, that is when he is with me the most. His is a most amazing kind of love.

LAWYER: But where is he, this Good Shepherd of yours? Where is your proof? Have you kept a log of the times he has laid down his life for you? Did you take pictures? Can you get a wolf in here to back up your claims? Because if you can't, sheep, this is all just hearsay.

SHEEP: You seem only interested in pasture-izing Jesus, making him easy to understand. You need to bring your whole self to this—your mind, body, and soul. I'm telling you, Jesus is my Good Shepherd. I'm alive because of him. I don't know how it happens but all we can say is, I'm a changed sheep because of him!

Heather Kirk-Davidoff and Nancy Wood-Lyczak

8

THE STORIED FIRES OF GOD

Words for Pentecost and the Weeks that Follow

M AY THE GRACE OF THE
LORD JESUS CHRIST BE WITH YOUR
SPIRIT, BROTHERS AND SISTERS.
AMEN.

Ephesians 6:18

Eternal Spark, on Pentecost let us celebrate the power of your spirit in creation and in us. You transform us, empower us, guide us, sustain us, and give us hope when we thought all was lost. We are touched by your flames and wind when we are moved to tears or laughter by a play or a book, when we listen to music that rocks our soul, when a friend takes our hand and shows us that love is action and not just a cozy feeling. Clothe our spirits in red and stir our wind chimes to melody today and always. Amen.

Susan Hodge-Parker

Opening Prayer · Acts 2:1–17

Glorious God, you blow into our lives without warning. With you we soar to a high peak in the realm Jesus knew, where we see with new eyes and hear with new ears a world bright with hope. As we walk our shadowed streets, let your Spirit dream within us the day when all will know your love and rejoice in your truth. Through Jesus Christ our Savior. Amen.

Kathryn J. Campbell

Invocation · Psalm 104

Whoosh! You Whoosher!
You fill the seas with playful whales
and our churches with irrepressible words.
Let us experience your Spirit
as adopting parent,
advocating counsel,
indiscriminate blesser,
so that we may babble our way
into understanding,
and kindle the wicks of many tongues
to flame a single faith. Amen.

Maren C. Tirabassi

Prayer of Approach (responsive)

We have heard about the storied fires of God:
fires that lead lost people in the wilderness at night,
and burn without consuming a green-leafed bush;
and come down from heaven on the wings of Elijah's prayer,
consuming the faint hearts of false prophets.

On this day of Pentecost,
it is the spirits of ordinary people that catch fire with joy,
consuming the attitudes and customs that divide them,
creating goodwill between them.

The Spirit that is Holy
appears in those who discover and delight in each other.

May it again be so! May such flames dance in us,
may we be on fire with the possibility of sharing life in love,
and may we spread this fire on!

Nancy Rockwell

Call to worship

O Most Holy God, we give you thanks that you are among us.
We thank you for the gift of your creation;
for the gift of friends and family;

for the gift of stories;

for the gifts of learning and knowledge;

for the gifts of question and doubt;

for the fire of enthusiasm;

for the wind of reason.

For all we understand, for all that remains a mystery,
for your loving presence in and through it all,

we give you thanks.

Jane O. Sorenson

CALLS TO WORSHIP—FIRST FIVE SUNDAYS OF PENTECOST

1

Spirit is in us.

We are in Spirit.

Spirit calls us to ministry.

Spirit calls us to prayer.

Spirit cries for peace.

Spirit works for justice. So do we!

2

Spirit is in our midst.

Spirit is in our hearts.

Spirit calls.

Spirit challenges.

Trust in the Holy One, for Spirit brings life.

Our hearts are open wide; our trust is true.

3

Spirit is with us and in us.

We are in Spirit.

Spirit heals.

Spirit comforts.

Spirit blesses our mourning with the oil of gladness;

And bestows on us a mantle of praise instead of a faint spirit.

Thanks be to God.

For grace abundant and love overflowing.

4

As the day dawns anew,

So do our spirits.

As our community gathers,

So does our joy.

As God's love awakens us,

Our hearts become one. And so it is!

5

Spirit comes!

Spirit blesses.

Spirit calls.

Spirit challenges.

Spirit challenges us to open our hearts and minds.

We open our lives to God's new directions.

June Goudey

Come, Holy Spirit

Speak in the swaying, swirling leaves,
that sing and dance in summer sunlight.
Whisper in the warm wind as I await your Word.
The silence speaks only of you,
holy sound sending
fickle, fleeting, fluttering shadows
like birds in flight,
calling out, singing, rejoicing in rhythmic refrain,
with spontaneity of Spirit.
O God, weave your Word of wholeness into our broken world.
Let us become patriots who act for you, for the poor, for all in need.
We hear the breeze of brokenness within and beyond our borders.

We hear the song of silent suffering
of the refugee, of rejection and resentment.
May we be vessels of reconciliation.
May we flee to you with our fragile, fragmented, fearful world.
We are made in your image! Is this your image?
We cry out with you, "No!"
May we shed sunlight where shadows of shame linger.
May we recognize our responsibility to the marginalized,
to those who dance in darkness:
The darkness of depression, despair, economic deprivation,
racism, sexism, and white privilege.
Open us to the cries of injustice.
Holy Spirit, move upon the waters of economic inequalities,
educational unfairness, health care dilemma,
that those who are "privileged" might use their power to empower
those struggling to make ends meet day by day,
to pay the bills, the rent, to pay for transportation, food, and clothing.
You who are the same yesterday, today, and tomorrow
let us not be content to stay the same
yesterday, today, and tomorrow.
Change us to fulfill your work.
Thy realm come . . . now.

Sue Henley

Invocation

Come, Holy Spirit, come. Renew your whole creation, nature and grace, soul and body, and all manner of matter. Move in and around us and fill us with your creative energy and extravagant light. May our hearts be open, may our hearts be stirred, for the work of love to which you call us and the hope of the world for which we labor. In Jesus' name. Amen.

June Goudey

Prayer for Illumination for the Season of Pentecost

God of grace and passion,
You sent the promised gift of the Holy Spirit
upon the apostles and the women,

upon Mary the mother of Jesus,
and upon his brothers.
Fill your church with power;
kindle flaming hearts within us
and cause us to proclaim your mighty works
in every tongue that all may call upon you.
We pray in the name and spirit of the risen Christ. Amen.

Jamie Norwich McLennan

Opening Prayer

Gracious God, you gather us here this summer morning as we welcome a new season. Your presence is made known to us in the beauty that surrounds us with flowers, birds, rain, and sunshine. Summer activities speak of life and joy in our community. And yet, as we look around and listen to the news, we recognize that all is not well with our world. We confess we sometimes wonder what it is we are called to do. Forgive our faltering faith and bless us, O God, with a spirit of discernment in our decisions, with compassion in our conversation, with love in our listening, with perseverance in our praying, and above all with hope that holds us in all seasons. Amen.

Sue Henley

Call to Worship for Trinity Sunday

Awesome, wondrous God,
dark, deep, and holy One,
we come to feel the mystery of your name.

**Green growing God,
Christ of many stories and disciples,
we come to hear the parable of your love.**

Bright, flashing God,
blowing wind and Holy Spirit,
we come to speak the gospel of your fire.

**Distant yet intimate God,
woven, puzzled, grained by time,
we come to find the Trinity of your grace.**

Maren C. Tirabassi

Confession · Mark 4:26–34

Mighty Planter God, you have thrown your seed on the ground that it might take root. You intended for us hope and abundance and new life. But, in our limited understanding, we have mixed some of our seeds in with your own— seeds of fear and bitterness, of greed and apathy. And then, even worse, seeing our mistakes, we have torn up the garden trying to make our garden "pure" again. We have pushed out our brothers and sisters, created laws that hurt and destroy, and built walls that isolate us from others and from ourselves. Forgive us our anxious weeding, O God, and help us to repair the garden of your heart. Show us how to cultivate a place of fruitfulness and hospitality, a place of grace and peace. And teach us trust, that we might leave the tending of the garden to your hand, and yours alone. In Christ's name we pray, Amen.

Anna Shirey

Prayer · Psalm 42; John 8:38

River of Life, for whom we thirst as the deer longs for the flowing stream, re- fresh us to new life by watering our dryness. Let us see your energy and power, which flow in everyday events. Become in us a stream of kindness, justice, and truth, for Christ's sake and for the sake of your beloved world. Amen.

Kathryn J. Campbell

LITURGY USING GENESIS 6, 7, 8

Opening Prayer

God, we embark in this sanctuary like refugees in an ark—for the storms of the week and the floods of our lives are close to drowning us. Here we shel- ter; here we make community with all people and all creatures. Gather us to- gether, then send us ashore with a benediction like a dove. Amen.

Call for Offering

Noah built the ark with pitch, lumber, and veterinary finesse. We build the church with gifts and talents, time and prayer. Let this offering be a symbol of all these.

Prayer of Dedication

God, bless these gifts that in this place shelter may be offered, diversity welcomed, hard times weathered, rainbows recognized. Amen.

Maren C. Tirabassi

Litany of God's Chosen · 1 Samuel 15:34–16:13

First I saw the strong and the mighty one, and I said to myself,

Surely this is God's chosen!

But God passed by. Then I saw the wise and the ancient one,
and I said to myself,

Surely this is God's chosen!

But God passed by. Then I saw the beautiful and the clever one,
and I said to myself,

Surely this is God's chosen!

But God passed by. Then came the small, the meek, the vulnerable one—
the child. And I said to myself,

Can this be God's chosen?

Can God see value in something so unimpressive, so insignificant,
so easily broken?

And God said "Yes!"

For while we see what's on the outside, God sees through to our souls.

ALL: We see with our eyes, but God sees with the heart.

Anna Shirey

Confession · 1 Kings 17:8–24

We confess, O God, that we have experienced the despair of the widow, looking at our dwindling resources and seeing no possibility of a future. In our anxiety we have hesitated to share our gifts with the Holy One in our midst, tempted to hoard what little we had. But, as we sympathize with the fear of the widow, inspire us also with her courage—she who, seeing only death, was still able to reach out for life. Teach us this lesson: when we submit to the miracle of faith, poverty is indeed transformed into abundance, and the practice of generosity creates new space for blessing. In Christ's name we pray, Amen.

Anna Shirey

Call to Worship · Psalm 9

The Blessed One is a stronghold of safety for those crushed by the world.
In every season of trouble, cling to this promise.
May this name be upon your lips in every waking hour.
In every storm of despair, hold fast to this assurance.
Let your voice resound with praise, for Creation's Song has yet to be silenced.
In every eruption of brutality, take refuge in this confidence.
The Faithful One will avenge every murderous impulse;
the cries of the afflicted ignite the Heart of Heaven.
When the gates of death are opened, fear not! Fear not!
The Advocate will never abandon. Another Way has opened.
A River of Peace shall be unleashed.
**ALL: Arise and arouse, O Christ, and roll back the rule of enmity. Amaze us
with your grace, so that all shall be well, and all shall be well, and all shall be
perfectly well.**

Kenneth L. Sehested

Confession · 1 Samuel 2:1–11; James 1:22–27

Divine Forgiver,
For our arrogant endeavors to live as islands,
and our willing ignorance of others . . .
God, have mercy upon us.
Giver of All Goodness,
For our greedy accumulation of wealth and prestige,
and our unlimited demands on this life . . .
Christ, have mercy upon us.
Granter of Purpose,
For our own ambitions devised pretentiously,
and our inflexibility to laugh and play . . .
God, have mercy upon us.

Rachel G. Hackenberg

Call to Worship

Let us pray together:

My soul praises you, O God!

Each of us gives thanks for the gift of life,
     for the having of this day.
Whether it brings us joy or sorrow, pain or ease,
     may we take it as a gift
          something to puzzle out or treasure,
          something that may lead us closer to you.

My soul praises you, O God!

Whether we sit alone or dance in the company of friends
     may we hear your Spirit calling to us:
          a call to faithfulness;
          a call to stillness, to work, to play;
          a call to prayer, to study, to silence.
          May we answer,

My soul praises you, O God!

Jane O. Sorenson

Litany of Fullness   ·   Isaiah 55:10–13

For God says, "I do not speak in vain.
My words do not fall on unyielding ground
and shall not return to me empty.
I speak with confidence.

My Word will return to me full of fruit.

My voice waters the earth, and my breath gives it life.
You who despair, look up in hope.
I speak with power.

My Word will return to me full of fruit.

My will is abundance; my intention for you
is courage and healing and grace.
I speak with compassion.

My Word will return to me full of fruit.

You shall go out with joy and be led back in peace.
All of creation will join in the dance of your celebration!

We are the fruit of your Word, and we return to you full.

Call to Worship · John 6:1–21

We gather in worship mindful of the need of the world.
We remember the hungry, the friendless, the homeless, the hopeless.
But we are only a few loaves and fishes. Are we enough?
We look out to the crowd ready, waiting,
needing nurture, praying that someone
might show them the good news of God's love.
But we are only a few loaves and fishes. Are we enough?
We hear the voice of Jesus instructing us
to break ourselves open,
to become vulnerable, available to the world around us,
to trust in God's promise of abundance.
But we are only a few loaves and fishes. Are we enough?
As we break ourselves open
we discover the fount of living water springing up within us,
the bread of healing and peace kneaded in our own hearts:
There is enough, enough for us and all the world.
Not only enough—more than enough.
ALL: With baskets of leftovers spilling onto the ground!

Anna Shirey

Litany of Laughter · Genesis 18:1–10a

When you told us to leave our old lives behind,
to set out on a path you would show us
and to put our trust in you,
We laughed in our fear.
We thought we might get lost.
When you told us we were special,
that you had chosen to bless us and lead us,
and bless the world through us,
We laughed in our astonishment.
We thought we were too ordinary.
When you told us you would make us fruitful,
that through us you would create blessings
numerous as the stars,

We laughed in our doubt.
We thought we were barren.
But when the promise was fulfilled,
and we held in our arms evidence of your love,
the power of your faithfulness,
We laughed in our joy, out loud!
We laughed because it filled us out,
 and poured out our souls—

ALL: And because we heard you laughing as well!

Anna Shirey

CONFESSION AND ASSURANCE
Ezekiel 2:1–5; Psalm 123; 2 Samuel 5:1–5, 9–10;
2 Corinthians 12:2–10; Mark 6:1–13

Invitation

We live in God's world,
but a world broken by our own doing.
God offers us wholeness,
yet we turn away,
refusing God's love
because it comes through means we dislike.
Let us confess our brokenness
and seek to be open to God's wholeness
though whatever means it comes.

Confession

Holy God,
we confess that we have sinned against you
and against your whole creation.
We have not loved you with our whole being;
rather we have loved ourselves at the expense of others.
We have ignored the cries of the poor.
We have turned away from those in need.
We have shunned those who are different from us.

We have abused and exploited each other
and the world you have made.
You have sent prophets to convict us of our sin,
yet we have rejected them.
Forgive us, O God.
Open our eyes, our ears, and our hearts
to your presence all around us.
Transform us in our weakness
to live with the power of the risen Christ,
accepting, loving, and serving all,
and living in harmony with all that you have made.
Amen.

Assurance of Grace

In our brokenness God is ever near.
In our time of need, God's love surrounds us.
We must simply be open to receive it.
Sisters and brothers,
God knows our brokenness
and God is here to bring healing and wholeness.
Receive the good news of God.
Through Jesus Christ we are forgiven
and by the Holy Spirit we are nurtured to wholeness.

Wesley Brian Jamison

9

THE WIDE WINDOW OF OUR SPIRITS

Words for Ordinary Time, or the
Second Half of the Season of Wind and Flame

THE GRACE OF THE LORD JESUS
BE WITH ALL THE SAINTS. AMEN.

Revelation 20:21

Opening Prayer for Any Season

Open wide the window of our spirits,
God, and fill us with light;
Open wide the door of our hearts
that we may receive and entertain you
with all our powers of adoration and love. Amen.

Jamie Norwich McLennan

fidelity · Matthew 14:23–33

what is this water walking, Jesus,
blue-brushed sky lowering toward

squint to cross the deepening,
God, you have for us something more?

thought at last the dream to sleep,
light receding, gone the shore

when you sudden wake the storm,
stirring, pulling into more!

urging us step clear the net,
risking life your waves to trace;

promise should we falter reach us,
turn your gale-blown night embrace.

William B. Jones

Responsive Confession and Assurance   ·   Matthew 14:22–33

We remember the great storm on Galilee, when Jesus' friends were rocked back and forth in their tiny boat of faith, and were frightened for their lives. Their friend came to them in their distress, but they didn't recognize him, thinking him a ghost.

How many times, O God, have we been blinded by our fear, and saw in your coming only the shadow of illusion?

We remember that Jesus approached the boat, and invited Peter to join him in standing on the waves. But Peter was afraid and lost sight of Jesus, and he began to sink.

How many times, O God, have we turned our attention to the distractions and anxieties of this world, and begun to sink into hopelessness?

We remember that Jesus had mercy on Peter and rescued him from the smothering waves, asking him why he had so little faith.

How many times, O God, have we cried out in our faithlessness, forgetting that you always rescue, you always save?

Even as we remember our faults, O God, we remember your mercy. And so we ask to be restored to your side, set back in the boat of your love, while the waves are calmed about us.

ALL: Master of the Wind, Lover of the Storm, Bringer of the Peace, teach us how to abide in you in all things.

Anna Shirey

Litany of God's Voice   ·   1 Kings 19:9–18

We stand on the mountain waiting for God to speak.
First comes a wind, a mighty and invisible force
that shakes us and knocks us to the ground.
Surely this power to overcome, that is God!

But God does not speak in the whirlwind.

Then comes an earthquake, a terrible rumbling and crumbling
beneath our feet that teaches us to kneel and cower.
Surely this power to subdue, that is God!

But God does not speak in the earthquake.

Then comes the fire, a terrible breathing dragon that licks our faces
and burns our eyes and makes us turn away and run.
Surely this power to terrify, that is God!

But God does not speak in the fire.

Then comes silence, stillness, peace.
Finally we hear God's voice.
It asks us only one thing, "Why are you here?"

We answer—To find our way home.

Anna Shirey

Prayer for Illumination for Any Season

Creator God—
We glory in the gift of your world.
May we love and trust you enough today
that we may open ourselves to hear your words
as they are written on our hearts
through scripture, word, and song. Amen.

Jamie Norwich McLennan

Loving God, we come to you for truth,
that we might see clearly and that we might understand.

**We come to you for comfort,
that we might be sustained and
that we might be understood.**

We come to you for challenge,
that we might be reminded that
our ways are not your ways and that we can change.

We come to you, Holy One. We come to you.

Jane O. Sorenson

∾

LITURGY · Psalms 34, 84; John 6:56–69

Call to Worship

How lovely is God's dwelling place.

**Our souls yearn for God's presence;
our hearts and our flesh cry out for the Living God.**

The Mighty One is a sun and a shield. God bestows favor and honor.

We seek God and God answers us. God delivers us from our fears.

Come into God's house. Here, even the sparrow finds a home,

even the swallow has a nest near God's altar.

Come all you who thirst, all you who are heavy laden. Come take refuge here.

Invocation

Eternal God, you are our shield; be present with us now. As we bring our broken hearts and crushed spirits, revive us. As we bring our joys and praises, exalt with us. We come broken and whole, sorrowing and rejoicing. You welcome us home. Thanks be to God. Amen.

Confession

Gracious God, we acknowledge that we have been feeding on a steady diet of quick fixes instead of dining on the spiritual fruits you offer us. We find it easier to nurture grapevines of gossip than to till the fields where you send us. We find it easier to promise than to produce. We realize that our steady diet of doing what is easiest has left our spirits malnourished. We feel empty and hollow deep inside. Forgive us our foolish ways. Amen.

Assurance of Grace

Know that God's grace as evidenced in the life of Christ Jesus is sufficient for us. Those who hunger and thirst for righteousness shall be fed. Thanks be to God.

Jean Helmer

Call to Worship · 1 Kings 8:1, 6, 10–11, 22–30, 41–43

We have made this place for you, O God, and gathered here to worship you.

But do you indeed dwell on earth?

Your presence floods into this sanctuary,
the fire of your Spirit settling on each of our heads,

But do you indeed dwell on earth?

Your presence flows into each of our lives,
filling our hearts with peace and our souls with song,

But do you indeed dwell on earth?

Even as we gather here in your presence, we acknowledge that your
dwelling place is not limited by our construction,
nor is your mercy limited by our needs.

But do you indeed dwell on earth?

On the earth, in the earth, and above the earth, in the depths of the
human heart and the depths of a single blade of grass: In every place we
can imagine, and places we cannot imagine,

ALL: And so we will meet you here, anywhere, and everywhere.

Anna Shirey

Gathering Words · 1 Kings 8:22–30; John 6:56–69

We come to this sanctuary entangled with the
worries of the world and our community . . .

The cost to repair our car
The images of war embedded upon our mind's eye
Whether or not the acolyte will light the candles properly
Why the microphone is not turned loud enough
Whether we will like the chosen hymns
What kind of muffins will be at coffee hour

We needed *one* more cup of coffee . . .

One more hour of sleep
One more obedient child
One more deposit in the bank
One more week of vacation
One more hour in each day
One more day in each week

As we roll our shoulders to relieve the stress, as
we lift our eyes to your holy altar, as we let go and let God,
remind us that you are *the One.*

With intention! we shake off our worldly cares,
turn our eyes to you in glad praise and trust your Spirit to
revive us again! Come on people, let us worship the One!

Let us pray
May worship be what nothing else is—a softening of the edges of doubt,
a tickling of God's great mystery upon our innermost being,
a wordless answer to the great questions of life,
a tender blowing of the Holy Spirit,
an assurance that there is a better way to live together on this planet
and that you, O God, are that way.

May your presence be palpable tonight, frothy and dancing,
alive with your great mystery.
May our voices in song impregnate the very air with grace.
May our prayers be authentic, heartfelt and healing.
May our tears be the morsels of confession that are just so good for the soul.

We are here with you.
We are together, and we are glad. Amen.

Judith K. Hanlon

Invocation · Song of Solomon 2:8–13

This text is oddly placed in the Revised Common Lectionary *in the northern hemisphre. We speak these praises recalling people of faith in the southern hemisphere.*

Listen! Listen for the sound of the Beloved, who comes leaping upon the mountains and bounding over the hills. Strain your ears for the sound of this voice.

Listen for the voice of our Beloved!

Behold the Beloved, standing like a gazelle behind our wall, gazing in at the windows, looking through the lattice.

Listen for the voice of our Beloved!

Our Lover speaks to us: "Arise, oh fair ones, oh fearful ones, oh weary ones, both long-faced and cheery ones, and come away with me."

Listen for the voice of our Beloved!

For lo, the winter is past, the flowers push through the cold and hardened soil. The time of singing has come. The fig puts forth bloom; the veins of the vine course with life; earth's fragrance fills the air.

Listen for the Voice of our Beloved!

ALL: O Lovely One, let me see your face, let me hear your voice. As sure as the day breathes and the shadows flee, I shall indeed arise and be joined with you, oh Lover of All Souls.

Kenneth L. Sehested

LITURGY BASED ON PSALMS 124, 125

Call to Worship

Those who trust in God are as secure as Mount Zion;
  they will not be defeated but will endure forever.

When the storms of life are raging, those who trust in God are secure.

If God had not been on our side when people attacked us,
they would have swallowed us alive in their burning anger.
The raging waters of their fury would have overwhelmed our lives.

When the storms of life are raging, those who trust in God are secure.

The wicked will not rule the land of the godly,
for then the godly might be tempted to do wrong;

When the storms of life are raging, those who trust in God are secure.

O God, correct us when we turn to crooked ways,
do good to those who are good, whose hearts are in tune with yours,

When the storms of life are raging, those who trust in God are secure.

ALL: Thanks be to God.

Invocation

We have come, O God, seeking you, seeking your presence, seeking your peace, seeking your fellowship. May we sense your presence here among us as we have gathered in this hour. Revive us again! Amen.

Confession

We confess that we often feel overwhelmed by life itself. We take actions that belie our faith in Jesus and the message of his grace. Deliver us from our doubts, O merciful God. Amen.

Assurance of Grace

Know that those who rely on God's grace cannot be defeated.
God loves us more than can be imagined—
in that love, we find peace.

Jean Helmer

Invocation · Matthew 19:13–15; Mark 10:13–16; Luke 18:15–17

O God, creator of this family,
    like willful children we disobey you;
    yet you open your arms to us with love and compassion.
Soften our hearts and warm our hands
    so that we may lead others to your embrace, saying
    "Children of God, you are welcome here."
May the grace of God, love of Jesus, and power of the Holy Spirit
    bless this time of worship.

Susan E. Brown

Opening Prayer · Matthew 10:16–30; Mark 10:17–31; Luke 18:18–30

Welcoming God, like weary camels through the gate called Needle's Eye we come. Help us to unburden ourselves so that we can walk through the door of your worship: unburden us of the desire for things that are not really us, of the striving with others that is not really us, of the feeling of constantly falling short that is also not us—strip these things away so we can be here, quietly, with our truest selves and with you. Amen.

Molly Phinney Baskette

꩜

PRAYERS OF CONFESSION FOR ORDINARY TIME

Confession

Generous God, we acknowledge our hearts are calloused and we shrug indifferently at both small kindnesses and great needs. We, of narrow hearts, are guilty of aimlessness and complacency. Enter into our smallness and grow our hearts wide with amazement that we have been blessed with your grace, bathed in your forgiveness. We pray in the name of the One who spat lukewarm water from his mouth, Amen.

Assurance of Grace

We are forgiven, washed, softened, pried wide open, enlarged . . . into grace.

Confession

God of Shining Clarity, we are so confused. We confuse having security with faith. We confuse sharing our excess with generosity. We confuse having with deserving. Restore us to our rightful minds. Help us know what riches we have and where we are poor indeed. Help us know true penitence and genuine gratitude. In the name of Christ, Amen.

Assurance of Grace

God's forgiveness untangles our confusion and makes us rich and poor at the same time. We are truly grateful.

Confession

Joyous Creator, from your Generous Self flows forth a world of brilliant beauty and amazing interdependence. You have honored us with the tasks of being caretakers and observing mirrors of this flaring river of deep life. Yet, we seek to control and own, and lose our place in our story. You came to liberate the captives, so set us free from the arrogance that holds us isolated from others in this shimmering web of life. In the name of the One who wore humility like a crown, Amen.

Assurance of Grace

God pulls us into web of all things. We discover that we are not trapped—we are connected. *God* crowns *us* with forgiveness, and we are amazed.

Confession

Loving God, you told us that to love you, our neighbors, and ourselves wa. to live the dance of joy. Created by Love, surrounded by Love, and made whole in Loving, we stumble. We do not believe in your infinite compassion for us. Forgive our doubt. We withhold unmerited forgiveness from each other. Forgive our desperate control. We despair we can ever love those who have hurt us. Forgive our shallow hope. Free us from the fears that hobble our steps. In the name of the Dancer, Amen.

Assurance of Grace

This is forgiveness—God takes our hands and leads us into the music of the world. We look around and everyone is dancing!

Priscilla L. Denham confessions; MCT Assurances

Opening Prayer

Holy God, who is both near and far,
    huge beyond measure
    and as tiny as a mustard seed:
to you we come.
We come to worship,
    to sing your praise
    to seek your help
    to learn your ways.
Help us to open our minds to all that you are:
    you contain all genders
        all melodies
        all colors
        all languages.
Our limited human understanding seeks to name
    who you are and how you are,
    and all our words and all our images fall short.
Keep us mindful, dear God, that our language may fall short
    but that you never do.
Holy God, to you we come.
Open our hearts and our minds to you.

Jane O. Sorenson

Responsive Prayer

I am filled with joy in knowing you.

I praise you at every turn because of your loving kindness.

I cannot help but praise you when I think what you have done for me.

What a delight to trust in you, O God,
From the depths of my soul
and the fullness of my heart I am blessed in your love.

Barbara Smith

Invocation

Almighty God, we have come to this place to find you; yet, you have been beside us all the time. Our prayer, then, does not so much ask for you to be here as it asks you to make our own hearts more aware of you. Creator, make an intentional and worshipful focusing of our minds a more constant discipline in our lives. Timeless as the sunshine, it is so easy to take your love for granted. Fill this moment with awe, loving God of our hope, and let us progress from a reverent hour into continual veneration, from a moment of devotion into a life of prayer. Amen.

Sheryl Stewart

Confession · Jeremiah 31:7–9; Mark 10:46–52

When we cloud the air with senseless words,

God have mercy.

When we bend your ear for our own greed, ignoring the needs of others,

God have mercy.

When we silence the cries for justice of those around us,

God have mercy.

When we ignore the voice of the Christ in our midst,

God have mercy.

When we fail to praise you with our words and actions,

God have mercy. Amen.

Donald Schmidt

Assurance of Grace

God clears the air, untangles the listening, lifts the tongue, pays attention, ignites our hearts—by free and festive forgiveness.

Maren C. Tirabassi

Prayer of Reflection and Confession

Holy One, I said "oops" this week:
I forgot to hold someone's hand;
I said the wrong thing to a friend in pain;
I didn't finish what I said I'd do;
I didn't look for you in the eyes of the stranger.

Holy One, forgive me my "oops"—
and help me to forgive others their "oops."
Wrap me up safe in your grace,
and give me the courage to keep on trying. Amen.

Jane O. Sorenson

Inside Out, A Litany

Love me from the inside out, God.
Take the thoughts I hide deep inside
and burn them with your purifying fire.

Love me from the inside out, God.

Take the roots of my mistrust and
deaden their hold on my life.

Love me from the inside out, God.

Take the thoughts that run freely in my mind
and trap them in your grace.

Love me from the inside out, God.

Take the hope you have planted in me
and nourish it with the support of the church.

Love me from the inside out, God.

Take the gift of the Spirit living in me
and ignite your love to lead me to your service.

Love me from the inside out, God.

Take your love in me
and let it infuse my living.

Love me from the inside out, God.

Arlene L. Drennan

MORE CONFESSIONS FOR ORDINARY TIME

Confession

God, we confess that sometimes we live between caffeine and tranquilizers—alternately trying to find energy for our lives or to relax enough to feel our own feelings. Forgive us the mood swings of the spirit, our misuse of body and soul, and the reaching outside of ourselves for the blessing you plant deep within. Forgive us, God, and detoxify our lives. Amen.

Assurance of Grace

In confession we make words of our faults and accept the full and amazing cleansing and healing of God's forgiveness. Thanks be to God.

Prayer of Confession

God, we confess our ordinary faults—the friend we did not call, the smile withheld, the road rage—real even if not verbal—the gossip spread, the unnecessary critical word, the time wasted, the new year's resolution already broken. Please forgive us and make us sensitive, aware, and caring, in Christ's name. Amen.

Words of Assurance

God forgives our great failings and our small infractions. God guides us into repentance and a change of heart.

Confession

O God, we confess—there was something kind we thought of doing, but it was too much effort. We knew a comment would hurt feelings, but it was so clever, we said it anyway. We were angry with a family member and dug up old shortcomings. We forgot "thank you" or "I'm sorry" to a child. We skipped the dog's walk, "stole" a parking space, ignored a lonely person, insulted a telemarketer. Forgive us not only our great sins, but also our disappointing fruit. Amen.

Assurance of Grace

Christ is our real time forgiver—knowing our pettiness and our failings and giving us each a new beginning in grace.

Confession

God, we confess that sometimes we close windows
    against the fresh air of new ideas,
    against the noise of other people's worries,
    against the winds of change.
God, we confess that we often draw the curtains
    against people who are different,
    against world news or community concerns.
Forgive us our insulation in our own homes,
    our shuttered churches,
    the security systems on our hearts.
Open up our lives. Amen.

Assurance of Grace

Forgiveness is the threshold. First we look out, then we are sent out . . .
Thanks be to God.

Maren C. Tirabassi

God Asks Us to . . . Open the Box

Don't limit my being;
untie the ribbon.
Don't restrict my presence;
remove the lid.
Don't be afraid to see what I am;
let me sit in your hands.
Don't keep me quiet;
let me use your voice.
Don't lead me in your ways;

let me guide you in our journey.
Don't harden your hearts;
let me grow in you and transform your life.

Open the box you keep me in;
let me open your life.

Arlene L. Drennan

Call to Worship (at times of departure)

How precious is your presence, God, in the comfort of this house of prayer.

Now that I will be going far away from this place, you have asked me to . . .

Call when I get there, and call every day,

Which really does mean, to promise that I will stay close;

For me it cannot be, call if I remember,

Or, call if it's convenient for me,

Or, call if I feel like it.

For although I know you will be available without me calling,

I also love and feel more secure when we exchange promises.

How precious is your presence, God, in every place I go.

Traveling, staying, enveloping God, wrap me as a cloak; make our car be like your shawl. Be with us while we spend long minutes in the car trying to find the right seating arrangement to squelch the sibling arguments, and while we spend long hours driving and riding. With you in our hearts, we are never alone. With all of us together, life is more precious. May your peace be in our preparations, our journey, our arrival. Amen.

David Pendleton and Abby Joy Pollender

Confession

Confession is an act of courage in response to hearing the Gospel preached. I invite you to become aware of truths that hurt so that God can use us as instruments of healing and hope. Let us pray:

Infinitely Loving One, God of our lives, we trust in you, but can you put your trust in us? You have made beauty that fades and returns to dust so that beauty might blossom anew. We have made soda bottles and fast food trays,

auto bodies and nuclear reactors that last beyond usefulness and then pois.
the earth. You have called creation a community to be loved while we have
seen it as a slave to be mastered. You have created abundance to be shared by
all that breathes, and we have stored resources while people starve. Forgive us
for not seeing, for despairing, for going along with the crowd. We long to
walk tenderly upon the earth, your body.

Silence

Assurance of Grace

By the power of love, God is able to renew a right spirit within us and grant
us courage to change our ways and challenge our culture of consumption.
In Christ Jesus we are a people renewed and forgiven. Thanks be to God!

Christina J. Del Piero

Call to Worship

Praise be to God
Praise be to God for the gift of life
Praise be to God for the gift of death
Praise be to God for the gift of hope
But, above all else,
Praise be to God for the gift of love
in which life and death and hope
are intermingled.
Praise be to God.

Prayer of Invocation

O Holy One, may this place be filled with your Spirit.
Gentle us into an unclenched moment,
    a deep breath,
        a letting go of heavy expectations,
            of shriveling anxieties,
                of dead certainties,
that, softened by your love,
    surrounded by your light,
        and open to your mystery,
            we may be found by wholeness,

upheld by the unfathomable,
entranced by the simple,
and filled with the joy that is you.

Amen

Roger Robbennolt

Prayer of Confession · Jeremiah 31:7–9; Psalm 126

Gracious and Loving God: You are ever faithful and yet we struggle to trust in you. While Ephraim yearned to return home from Babylon, your face never turned away. Likewise you never abandon us . . . but our hearts are slow to trust. "I will bring them back," you promise. "I will lead them beside still water . . . they will not stumble . . . because I am Israel's Father." We read and *know* you are faithful to your Word, yet we are too ashamed to accept your promise to abide within us and among us, to preserve and protect us. Forgive our disbelief, fear, hesitance to accept you at your Word. Amen.

(Time of silent, personal confession)

Assurance of Grace

"The Lord has done great things for us and we are filled with joy." Like those returning from Babylon, "the ones who sow in tears will reap with songs of joy." Of this we can be certain—for our God is completely trustworthy!

Dianne Kiesz

Musical Response Following Psalm 126

Choir/congregation: "The Lord has done great things for you and me."
Voice 1: *four syllables (see examples)*
Voice 2: *four syllables (see examples)*
Choir/congregation: "and we all laughed and sang."

Examples:

THEME	VOICE 1	VOICE 2
Spring/nature	Cool soaking rains	Grey geese flew north
Wedding anniversary	William and Joy	Wed fifty years
School	Children are glad	First day of school
Traveling	Journeyed afar	Home safe and sound

Channice E. Charles

Invocation · Ruth 1:1–18

We are your people—no matter the circumstances of our lives in past or present times. There are many options before us, but not all lead to the abundance of life you have to offer. May we cling to your promise that you are always there with us. Wipe away our tears and give us the joy of your love. Open our spirits to the possibilities of new faith experiences. Amen.

Elaine Miller

Responsive Reading—A Beatitude · Psalm 146

Blessed are those imprisoned . . .

God will set them free.

Blessed are the blind . . .

God will bring light to their eyes.

Blessed are those who are shoved down by life . . .
God will lift them up
Blessed are those living outside mainstream society . . .

God will gather them up and bring them in.

Blessed are those who are left alone, left with no family or friends . . .

The Holy One will call them children of God.

Kristi McLaughlin

Prayer for Halloween

On this hallowed evening, may the Holy Spirit fill us with the tricks of the trade of mask-making. In the same way that you call us to imagine ourselves in others' shoes, call us to try on the faces, the masks, the voices, and the characters of those who fascinate and captivate us, those whom we fear, those whom we adore, those who have gone before us. Guide little ones, elders, and everyone in-between safely as they cross paths with strangers, knock on neighbor's doors, and open their own front doors. Tonight is a thin place—where darkness and light, heaven and earth, life and death, fear and awe dance so closely together. Saint us, trick us, betwixt us, treat us, beg us, and hallow us as we hallow your name.

Elizabeth D. Barnum

Invocation

Dancing God, exuberant, playful God, you who seem to wear masks and then come to us unmasked as pure warmth, love, and energy, you who strip away our masks leaving us vulnerable, real, and renewed, we thank you for the mystery of life, for the mystery of our aliveness. Be close to us; take our hands and lead us in your Spirit-filled dance. Amen.

Christina J. Del Piero

Samhain (for B.A.R.) for All Hallows, All Saints, and All Souls

Outside my window,
scarlet and orange maples
burn in a last explosion of light.

On Samhain,
when Celts lit bonfires on hilltops,
flames leapt to the sky
burning into darkness.

Shadows against firelight,
the dead
come to visit the living,
the veil between worlds, thin.

In the morning, after the fires
burned down
great clouds of smoke lifting
from the hills, billowed across the sky,
extinguishing the light.

Anne Dewees

Saints (All Saints' Day)

God, for all the saints I give you thanks—
for grandparents and godparents,
for doctors and teachers,
for coaches and pastors.

God, for all the saints I give you thanks—
for authors of books that have moved me,

for friends whose advice has guided me,
for strangers who proved an example,
for my children and the children of others
who have given me courage.

God, for all the saints I give you thanks—
for those nearest and farthest away,
for those who have died,
and those who are living,
for those who knew they made a difference
and those who never will.

God, for all the saints I give you thanks. Amen.

Maren C. Tirabassi

Thanksgiving Call to Worship

Come, you thankful people, come.
Let us gather before God and lift up our songs of praise and thanksgiving.

God our maker does provide for our wants to be supplied.
Let us give thanks for God's generous spirit.
Let us give thanks for the blessings of food and family, of church and faith.
Let us give thanks for the beauty of the earth.

Let us praise God from whom all blessings flow.

Susan J. Foster

Opening Prayer—Thanksgiving Day/Season   ·   Psalm 95

Wondrous Spirit, we raise to you our joyful noise: words of thanksgiving, songs of praise! Rhythm-setter of tides and seasons, from the depths of the waters to the heights of the land, creation declares your greatness. You dapple our days with sun and our nights with starlight. Unceasingly flow your love and peace. May your goodness transform us, deepening our gratitude for the beauty around us, the kindness among us, the bread broken for us. Lead us, we pray, in blessing the lives of others, so that all your world may have reason to rejoice. Amen.

Ann B. Day

Thanksgiving Prayer

Gracious God, Source of all Blessings,
You have been extravagant in your Generosity.
You have planted within us the seeds of Hope.
You have nurtured within us the saplings of Faith.
You have harvested the fruits of your Creation and
spread before us the feast of all Possibility.

Words cannot express the gratitude with which
we come before you.

May we embody our thanks with extravagant generosity.
May we offer our lives to you in acts of compassion for one another.
May we walk gently upon the earth, ever mindful of your gifts
of Breath, of Love, of Life itself. Amen.

Anne G. Cohen

10

NAAN, KHLEP, WELCHES, AND NAPA MERLOT
Words for Communion

[JESUS] SAID TO THEM, "THIS IS
MY BLOOD OF THE COVENANT, WHICH IS
POURED OUT FOR MANY. TRULY (AMEN)
I TELL YOU, I WILL NEVER DRINK AGAIN
OF THE FRUIT OF THE VINE UNTIL
THAT DAY WHEN I DRINK IT NEW
IN THE REALM OF GOD."

Mark 14: 24-25

Communion Invitation · Jeremiah 17:8; Joshua 1:9; John 15:9–17

For a tree to flower and bear fruit it must be
　　planted in the proper soil,
　　showered with water,
　　and warmed with the sun.
We, who want to fulfill the will of our Creator,
　　seek the solid ground of God,
　　the living water of Jesus Christ
　　and the radiant light of the Holy Spirit.
We come to this table tonight,
　　at the invitation of the Risen One.

Susan E. Brown

We affirm the goodness of life and the openness of the future because our God is a God of life and love. As God comes to us in this act of communion with one another, let us go out to others in Jesus' name. May our every prayer be an action that brings healing, reconciliation and hope to a broken and hurting world. Amen

June Goudey

INVITATIONS FOR PARTICULAR SEASONS OF THE CHURCH YEAR

Advent Invitation

Long ago and far away, village shepherds were tending their flocks one winter evening, dimly aware of ancient promises and a lingering hope they hardly understood. Suddenly light shone in the darkness, and the air was full of unexpected news. Confused and frightened, they knew that everything was different now, though nothing had actually changed.

So they went to Bethlehem, which means "place where bread is baked." There they saw a Child who owned nothing but a name. And it was good bread to them, the sight of the Child.

Like them, we remember ancient hopes and wonder what they mean, or if they could be real. Like them, we are frightened by sudden disturbances and unexpected news. The world is older now, but nothing has seemed to change. We are still uncomfortable with angels. Yet we leave our houses and routines to come to this place, where Baked Bread has been placed in promise of Bethlehem.

We, too, have had glimpses of holiness, and we are nourished by them. At this table we claim the food of sacred stories and of our own lives, remembering how it is that ordinary people find angels.

Epiphany Invitation

The presence of the Spirit comes to us with unexpected brightness, often answering unspoken prayers. Any light, a winter window, an open door, a table candle, the evening star, can be a palpable sign of God's presence, calming our fears, strengthening our resolve, protecting us from despair.

And still we seek an Inner Light for our inward bleakness, still we long to know the shining of the Risen One among us, with us.

Gathered here, we risk the hope that people with God's light in them can re-make their lives with a bit of bread and a shared cup; that nothing is lost forever; and that nothing is impossible with God.

We seek a connection beyond understanding, a gleam of holiness in the Bread of the Promise and the Cup of Joy.

Holy Week Invitation

Long ago the companions of Jesus went with him into Jerusalem. Among them were Thomas, a man given to grave doubts, Mary, a woman who longed for a different ending, Peter, who liked simple solutions, and Judas, whose bitterness was growing day by day.

Sensing danger everywhere in that time and place, they listened anxiously as Jesus spoke to them about generosity, abundance, sorrow, and love.

We still experience confusion, in our times. We waver and try to find a way out. Jesus is as hard to understand now as then.

Aware of our limits, and of Jesus' strength, we come to this table, knowing hard times are at hand, and opening our hands to God, who gives us what we need, in our times.

The Table of the Good Shepherd

We have heard about the Good Shepherd's Feast of Rejoicing.

We have heard that all people are welcomed to this bread and this cup, both old and young, the rich and the poor, in every language and race, and in many differing prayers.

The Good Shepherd's bread and cup—
We praise God for the extraordinary peace and power that is in them.

Always consumed, they are still eternal in their presence.

From them we make the vitality of each day's loves, tears, sorrows.

By them we are made new every day.

In them we can taste heaven.

Through them comes the power of Easter, and strength for the journey of life. We reach for the stars and walk the good earth, sustained by this Bread and Cup.

The table welcomes us, in Jesus' name.

Nancy Rockwell

FOR WORLD COMMUNION SUNDAY

Bring different breads; decorate the table with fabric clearly woven in another country.

Invitation

In India right now, the Christians are tearing naan. In Russia, the Orthodox are blessing khlep. In Ohio, they are pouring the Welch's. In California they are sipping some fine Napa merlot. But no matter how we break it, slice it, cube and dice it, this bread and this cup somehow make us one. If we can't see it, let us trust that Someone can. If we don't believe we are faithful or believing enough to take it, let us trust that Someone is, and invites us along. Let us not be broken any more, one from another. It is ready, and offered for all.

Prayer of Consecration

Our God, you welcome us to this table, people of every religious tradition: Roman Orthodox Episcometholutherbaptist Unitarians—as well as people who are finding meaningful faith for the first time. Bless us, bless this meal; may it start yet another conversation in our hearts, as you become more real for us.

Words of Institution

I want to offer the words of institution in Latin, the language that gave birth to so many others, to the babble of romance languages from Italian to French to Spanish—if these words are unintelligible, let that remind us that what we do is, in fact, a mystery.

"Ibi enim suas in manus panem sumpsit Christus quem fregit discipulisque dedit dicens: "Accipite, comedite: hoc est enim corpus meum, quod pro vobis datur."

Deinde calicem in manus vini sustulit eisque dixit: "Accipite et bibite omnes: hic calix novum aeternumque testamentum est in sanguine meo, qui pro vobis funditur et pro omnibus in remissionem peccatorum.

Thanksgiving

Along each of our journeys we've picked up snippets of people, and snippets of language. Let us bring the crumbs of the loaf back together. Hark back to ninth-grade French class, or the bit of Welsh or Italian or Nigerian you learned from your grandmother: remember, if you can, how to say "thank you" in a language other than English. Shout it aloud, the Eucharist, the thanksgiving! Say it more than once! *Gracias. Grazie. Merci. Spacibo.*

Molly Phinney Baskette

Great Thanksgiving, Worldwide Communion

The Lord be with you.

And also with you.

Lift up your hearts.

We lift them up to the Lord.

Let us give thanks to the Lord our God.

It is right to give our thanks and praise.

It is truly right and good to glorify you,
At all times and in all places, O God.
Through your living word you created all things
And pronounced them good.
You made human beings in your own image,
Persons capable of entering into relationships
Both with you and with each other.
From Abraham and his wives Sarah and Hagar
You brought forth nations of peoples.
As Abraham opened his tent and shared hospitality
You have shared of your grace with these nations.
Through prophets, rabbis, and teachers
You have sought to be in loving relationship
Even when we have sought to go our own ways.
You have called us as sisters and brothers to be a great family
We have brought others pain and heartache
And yet you offer us a way of reconciliation.
So today we join with all your people on earth
Praising your name in unending song, saying:

Holy, Holy, Holy Lord, God of power and might,
Heaven and earth are full of your glory.
Hosanna in the highest.
Blessed is the one who comes in the name of the Lord.
Hosanna in the highest.

In the fullness of time you sent the Chosen One,
Jesus of Nazareth, the Christ, your own,
To call your splintered creation together again.
He came preaching repentance and forgiveness of sins
And to those who responded he announced
They are joint heirs of eternal love with him.

When the stubborn forces of evil
Threatened to bring his life to an end,
He called his followers together
And took the bread, broke it, and said:
"Take, eat, this is my body broken for you."
Then he passed the cup and invited all,
"Drink from this, it is my blood of the new covenant.
Do this in remembrance of me."
Now on this day, his followers all around the world
Are gathering at table to remember and share,
And we are among those who are coming to this feast of love.
In remembrance of these your mighty acts in Christ,
We offer ourselves in praise and thanksgiving
As a holy and living sacrifice,
In union with Christ's offering for us,
As we proclaim the mystery of faith.

Christ has died. Christ is risen. Christ will come again.

O holy God, Creator of all people and worlds,
Send now upon this bread and cup
Your life-giving Spirit.
May this outpouring of the promised Spirit
Transfigure this thanksgiving meal
That this bread and this cup
May become for us the body and blood of Christ.
As we partake of this holy meal,
Fill us with the Holy Spirit
That we may be one body and one spirit in Christ.
All glory and honor is yours, almighty God,
Now and for ever.

Amen.

David Schmidt

A Grace

Creator of the stars and skies,
Our Protector as we rise;
Caught, as we are, in the web of time,

Strengthen us through bread and wine.
Enshrouded by the fall of night
Reveal to us eternal light.
Amen.

Roger Robbennolt

Prayer for Communion

Realizing that we are not perfect, O Potter,
we come asking that you shape us and mold us.
Guide us and help us to choose the harder right
instead of the easier wrong.
We accept the invitation to your supper.
Though we may be broken or imperfect,
we come seeking to be new creations in Christ Jesus. Amen.

Barbara Smith

Invitation to Communion (responsive or two leaders) · Luke 14:1–24

Who would we invite for dinner, if we could choose the people?

I know who would be invited to our table.

People we have never met, whose lives impressed us from the stories we heard or read.

People with whom we could play games or sing songs or discuss the very many different ways of life.

People and pets that wandered off without much, if any, explanation.

Foreigners, because they are the people who could never get here.

People in our own home, because they are the people who are seemingly always going to be here.

Fictitious people and characters from books, movies, comics, and cartoons.

Writers, musicians, priests, CEOs, princesses, and paupers.

Christ invites to this table.

David Pendleton and Abby Joy Pollender

Invitation

We have heard about God, who loved confusion into order and gave each creature a divine image, making the world.

We have heard about Jesus, a poor man whose banquet feeds the world, a healer whose wounds give life, a teacher whose wisdom traces love's order in the world, finding the divine in each of us.

We have heard how Jesus died, and how, for those who loved him, he rose again.

We have heard about the Holy Spirit, who breaks the bonds of race and class, of gender and creed, to show God's love for everyone.

And we have heard that love makes all things new.
We come to this table asking for the bread of such blessings.

These miracles begin with simple human gestures, bits of bread in a basket, tongues that talk, souls that yearn. And so we bring bread and wine, prayers and our own yearning, that the miraculous may begin in us today.

Nancy Rockwell

LITURGY FOR THE BEACH · John 2, 21

Invitation

As Christ is the host of this meal, there is no guest list, no engraved invitations, no formal dress required—for it is a given that all who desire communion with him, and community with each other, are welcome to this feast. Come, as Peter did, with joy to meet the Teacher, for all things are ready.

Prayer of Consecration

A simple loaf, a cup of juice. And yet so much more: a bridge between solid land and shifting sea; between us and you, God, between something less real and something more real. Our substance is not changed, just as the bread remains bread and the juice juice, and yet all three take on a new meaning in this meeting. Reveal our true substance as you reveal the real purpose of this bread and this cup: reveal us as the kind of people with whom Jesus would want to share breakfast.

Words of Institution

Christ's first miracle in John's gospel was to give us something to drink: the water into wine at the wedding in Cana. His last was to give us something to eat: a fish fry on the beach. From beginning to end, he feasts us. No less a feast was the solemn assembly on Jesus' last living night on earth, when he took a loaf at the Passover meal, blessed it, and broke it, and shared it out among his disciples saying "Take, eat, this is my body, which is broken for you. Do this to remember me."

Likewise after supper Jesus took a cup, and when he had given thanks to God for it, shared it out among all his disciples saying, "This is the cup of the new covenant, my blood, which is poured out for many for the forgiveness of sins. Do this, as often as you drink of it, to remember me."

Thanksgiving

O God, we thank you for knowing when we are hungry, before we ourselves know it. We thank you for the friendship of Christ that has a meal ready for us when we are weary with the long night's working and have come up empty, powerless to provide for ourselves. Grant us the humility and enthusiasm to keep coming back to warm our hands around this campfire, Christ's feast of love, now, and in all our days. Amen.

Molly Phinney Baskette

All His Friends

He serves real food:
For skeptics it's unexpected sustenance,
For whisky priests an embarrassment of grace,
For all us sinners our first square.

And with it always a quick stab to the heart:
Watch him rip the loaf, lift the cup,
Speak his grief—his chest heaving.

He addressed them as friends. That is what he called Judas
When that disciple
Betrayed him in the garden with a kiss.

Ah, friends—they can eat your bread and plan your undoing.

At the end of the meal when, as scripture says they sang a hymn,
Did Jesus sing too?
    Could he, knowing all that had been done and undone?

Yes, I think so. I think he sang the blues. He had before:
"Oh, Jerusalem, you who stone the prophets, how often would I have gath-
ered you in my arms as a hen her chicks,
But you would not."

The blues means not knowing how to stop loving when loving hurts.
It's what makes Jesus a Billie Holiday fan—
A broken heart that keeps on singing.

And when she wailed, or softly moaned into the mike,
Weighed down by her regrets, trapped
By life's always speculative investment in other human hearts,
Could she hear him say,

"Close out your set, my beloved. Come down from that hazy stage, and join
me at
    My table. I've ordered a meal for you."

David Slater

cast off

to compare and contrast no longer the lives
I have not had with this one:

not larger, more noticed
nor quieter, steadier

not better accompanied
nor less attached,

not gifted more
nor costed less,

just this life,
this one life

to take
and eat
and know.

William B. Jones

Reflections on Communion

Words of reflection on the bread: The bread is symbolically
broken body of Christ; however, as a staple food in ancient times
resented life itself. Jesus said, "I am the bread of life" (John 6:35) so we may
offer this image of bread as the living Christ healing the body, cleansing the
emotions and mind, and activating the soul.

Bread is also made up of the crushed grains of wheat, grown in the rich
earth and nourished by the sun and rain, harvested and made by human
hands. It contains the invisible agent of leaven, which transforms the dough,
doubling it in size to serve many. So too, does the Holy Spirit act like invisible
leaven in our lives to transform us into something larger so that we may serve
many. All of God's creation participated in the making of this bread so we, as
we partake of it, become one with God, Christ, and all of God's creation.

The purpose of bread is to feed and nourish others. It does no good to
sit on a plate and look attractive. In order for it to fulfill its purpose, bread
must be broken and given to others. So, like Christ, are we to be broken open
to serve others as part of fulfilling our purpose.

Words of Reflection on the Juice: Similar to the bread, the wine/juice traditionally symbolizes the lifeblood of Christ poured out for us. Jesus told his disciples that the cup was the new covenant they were to have with God and that
each was to drink from the cup. We can consider another symbol of the juice
as the regenerating spirit of Christ renewing his presence within us, infusing
and strengthening our own life force. When we, as a chalice, empty ourselves,
we are ready to receive the outpouring of God's grace and forgiveness.

The juice is also a combined product of all God's creation. Note how neither the juice nor the bread resemble the original "fruit" that was harvested.
Each has changed and become something more than it was in the beginning.
Each loses its individual identity and blends with the greater community to
become one as we become one with Christ. When we come to God's table,
we ask God's blessing on the ordinary gifts of the earth—the bread and the
wine/juice—and we also ask God to take our ordinary lives and transform
them for extraordinary work in God's world.

Susan Hamilton

Maybe Mystery

A miniscule morsel
    (in my hand a sacred moment)
      magnifies
      the tiny, three-year tale of hope
      into a cosmic
        (well-nigh comic)
      act
      of overcoming darkness.

A foolish, flawed cup
    (filled with store-bought juice)
      draws society's cynicism—
      yet,
      it is thrust up in the face of madness
      and we are promised
      sanity
      of the spirit.

It may be
    (as we are intimately involved in the guesswork
    of the Holy Ghost)
      that
      we stand
      in the
      Presence
      of
      healing Mystery.

Roger Robbennolt

∿

COMMUNION IN TIMES OF NATURAL DISASTER

Invitation

How can we eat our bread when we know there are others, far away, who are hungry? How can we drink our juice when we think of our brothers and sisters whose mouths are parched for lack of clean water?

When Jesus first offered this meal to his disciples, it was to enlist them in the final suffering and victory: not to deny that bad things happen to good people, but to say that we share in everything we have, and everything that happens to us. We come to this table today to do exactly that—to remind ourselves that we are inextricably part of all the things and people of creation, of the seed and grape that grew into this meal, of the men and women and children who labor to rebuild their villages and their lives on the other side of the world. Let us not hold back, but join them.

Consecration

As you bless this meal, God, bless us too—make us a living meal, our substance and our attention in prayer poured out for your many children who are struggling for life. Hold us together in the invisible communion of the spirit. Amen.

Thanksgiving

God who makes all things new,

We thank you for letting us come as we are and share in this meal. We know that we are what we eat, and, having taken into ourselves the body and blood of Jesus, we gain his power, his healing abilities, his commitment to justice for all people. Help all of us gathered here to work together as the different parts of the body of Christ—hands, eyes, voice, and conscience—to carry on Christ's work and witness and worship. *Amen.*

Molly Phinney Baskette

Communion Prayer · Jeremiah 31:7–9

We come, O Christ, from the lands of the north
From lands ravaged by drought,
lands scorched by prairie wild fires,
lands swept by relentlessly harsh winds.

Restore us at your table, Christ.

We come, O Christ, stumbling along uneven paths,
blinded by doubts, limping with fatigue;

Restore us at your table, Christ.

We come, O Christ, scorched and ravaged,
blind and lame, barren and expectant

Restore us at your table, Christ.

Knowing all are welcome at your table, we come,

Restore us at your table, Christ.

Jean Helmer

Service of Communion For Women Survivors of Violence

John 1; Song of Solomon 6, 7, 8; Mark 14,15; Proverbs 8, 9; Wisdom of Solomon 7:22–8:1; Ecclesiastes 1:4

God is within you.

And also in you.

Open your hearts to God's loving presence; trust in God's goodness.

We open our hearts to the One who is utterly trustworthy.

Let us give thanks to God,

For God's love has transformed us and made us whole.

We praise you, O God, mother and father of all creation,
For out of darkness and chaos, you brought light and life,

And called it good.

You are present at the beginning, in the middle, and the end of times,
so no matter where we are in our journey,

You are there.

How do we address you? We speak to you as Sophia,
the Wisdom of God, of whom it is written:
There is in her a spirit that is
intelligent, holy, unique, manifold, subtle,
mobile, clear, unpolluted, distinct,
invulnerable, loving the good, keen,
irresistible, beneficent, humane, steadfast, sure,
free from anxiety, overseeing all.
She is a breath of the power of God,
and a pure emanation of the glory of God;
therefore nothing defiled gains entrance into her.
For she is a reflection of eternal light,
a spotless mirror of the working of God,
and an image of God's goodness.

Although she is but one, she can do all things,
and while remaining in herself, she renews all things;
in every generation she passes into holy souls
and makes them friends of God, and prophets.
Against wisdom, evil does not prevail
She reaches mightily from one end of the earth to the other,
and she orders all things well.

Holy, holy, holy God of love and wisdom and light,
The whole universe sings your praise.
Blessed is the one who comes bearing wisdom's name!
Blessed is the light that shines in the darkness, full of grace and truth.

In the company of Mary and Elizabeth, you came,
O Wisdom, to dwell in Jesus of Nazareth.
In Jesus, you brought healing and life—
to Simon's mother-in-law,
to the woman who touched the hem of your garment,
to the little girl, twelve years old, whom you restored from the dead,
to the Syro-Phoenician woman and her daughter,
to the children you blessed, refusing to send them away,
to the widow whose offering you praised,
to the woman with her alabaster jar, who anointed you with oil,
to the "many other women" who came up with you to Jerusalem,
to Mary, your friend and confidant,
and Mary the mother of James and Joseph, and Salome,
who watched as you died,
and who were the first to witness your transformation.

You are the light that cannot be overcome by darkness,
You are the bringer of life, the life that is the light of all people.
But in Jesus you are also a bruised reed, and a person of sorrows.
You know what it is like to be despised and rejected,
mocked and spit upon,
stripped and falsely accused;
to feel betrayed and deserted by those closest to you
and to feel forsaken, even by God.
And so you gather us to you, as he did on that night so long ago:

While they were eating, he took a loaf of bread, and after blessing it he broke
it, gave it to them, and said, "Take, this is my body." Then he took a cup, and

after giving thanks, he gave it to them, and all of them drank from it. He said to them, "This is my blood of the covenant, which is poured out for many. Truly I tell you, I will never again drink of the fruit of the vine until that day when I drink it new in the realm of God."

And so in gratitude for God's wisdom, and in remembrance of the one who overcame betrayal and suffering and death, we offer ourselves in union with Christ and proclaim the promise of transformation.

Love was dead. Love was restored. Love lives again.

Now may we feel your Spirit in us and among us. Gather up everything in us that was forsaken and reclaim it as your own. Make this bread and this wine be for us the means of transformation and recovery, that the spirit of wisdom may dwell in us as a breath of the power of God: holy, unique and manifold, unpolluted, making us an image of God's goodness, renewing us, passing into our souls and making us friends of God and of the prophets, that we may in turn befriend the wounded and speak prophetically of God's transforming justice and love. Amen.

In the broken bread we participate in life of Christ.

In the cup, we participate in the new life Christ brings.

Thanksgiving

We give thanks, loving God, for the bond of this ritual that links us in solidarity to all who have called upon your name. May your wisdom grow within us. Send us out into the world as women of courage, compassion, and commitment. Amen.

Jeanyne Slettom

Unexpected Guests at the Communion Table

The sanctuary is ready for communion, with the elements still covered. Two aliens enter from the rear, up the center aisle, talking and looking around as they go. Zack, Raelyn and Sarah/Sam (depending on cast) are in middle school

ZIPZOR: So this is earth, huh? Kinda nice so far. Buildings, wildlife, friendly humanoids.

ORBITUS: Yeah, yeah, yeah. I see all that. But after a couple of million light years, all I really want is something to eat. We can scope it out later. I'm hungry!

ZIPZOR: *(disgusted)* You're always hungry.

ORBITUS: *(pointing to the communion table)* What's that up ahead? I think I see food! Come on! *(hurries toward table, gets ready to grab something)*

ZACK: *(standing up and coming forward)* Hey, you! Who are you? And what are you doing at our communion table? *(Raelyn and Sarah/Sam also come forward.)*

ZIPZOR: Uh-oh.

ORBITUS: Who, me? Uh, well, it looked like food and I was hungry and, well, I thought I might just have a bite or two and uh . . .

RAELYN: You don't look familiar to me. Have we met before?

ZIPZOR: Greetings, earthling. I am Zipzor, celestial pioneer from the galaxy Krytonia, and this is my copilot Orbitus. We have come across many miles and many galaxies to visit Earth. We bring you greetings in the name of the Krytonian people.

(Orbitus begins moving behind the table)

SARAH/SAM: *(surprised)* Well, uh, good to meet you, I guess. Welcome to Earth. And welcome to St. Luke's. No matter who you are or where you are on life's journey, you're welcome here—I guess that means aliens too.

ORBITUS: Great! Thanks! Now how 'bout some chow? Space travel really makes a guy hungry! *(Reaches to uncover the communion bread)*

ZACK: Wait! What are you doing? You're not supposed to touch that! That's for communion!

ORBITUS: *(Ignoring Zack, lifting off lid of communion bread and looking inside)* What have we here? Protein pods? Melting sponge meals? Hunger absorbent tissues? I don't care what it is, I'm hungry!

RAELYN: It's communion bread—you can't just eat the communion bread!

ORBITUS: Watch me!

ZIPZOR: Orbitus, listen to them! Put that down! *(Orbitus makes a disappointed, frustrated face, but puts the lid down.)* Is it poisonous or something?

SARAH/SAM: Of course it's not poisonous. It's just special.

ZIPZOR: Oh, I understand. Magic bread. What does it do? Give you strength? Or power? A love potion? Maybe makes you invisible?

ZACK: No, it's not magic, it's just special. It belongs to Jesus, and we share it with everyone.

ORBITUS: Everyone? You mean all these people? Then it had better be pretty filling, because I'm starved.

RAELYN: You don't eat communion bread because your stomach is hungry. You eat it because your soul is hungry.

ZIPZOR: A hungry soul? What's that?

SARAH/SAM: I think we'd better start from the beginning, guys.

ZACK: Sounds like a good idea.

RAELYN: Alright, the beginning. There was a man, well, mostly a man—he was also the Son of God, and he came to earth more than two thousand years ago.

ZIPZOR: What planet was he from? Maybe we know him.

ORBITUS: Did he get to eat the communion bread?

SARAH/SAM: He wasn't from outer space. He was from heaven, from God. And his name was Jesus.

ZACK: And he invented communion bread.

ORBITUS: Ah, a chef!

RAELYN: No, not a chef. A teacher, a prophet, a leader. Jesus was sent by God to teach us God's ways here on earth. He lived for about thirty years, and during that time he taught the people around him how to live in peace, to love one another and to follow God. He also performed healings and miracles.

SARAH/SAM: Yes, but some people didn't like what Jesus had to say, and they plotted against him. They had him arrested and tried and killed, crucifying him on a cross.

ZIPZOR: What a sad story!

ZACK: Oh, but there's a happy ending—after he died, Jesus came back to life. God resurrected him to prove once and for all that good triumphs over evil and God won't stop loving us, no matter what.

ORBITUS: So is that where the bread comes in? Bringing people back to life?

RAELYN: On his last night with his followers, just before his arrest and crucifixion, they all sat down to dinner together.

ORBITUS: Oh, so there's dinner involved? Now I'm listening!

RAELYN: (continuing) After they had eaten the meal, Jesus picked up the bread and broke it and gave them each a piece. He told them, "This is my body, broken for you. Do this in remembrance of me."

ORBITUS: *(horrified and grossed out)* Eeew! So this isn't bread, it is flesh. You're cannibals!

SARAH/SAM: No, it's symbolic. This is just bread. *(To Raelyn)* Keep going.

RAELYN: Then he picked up the cup of wine and told them, "This is my blood, shed for you. Do this in remembrance of me."

ZIPZOR: Please tell me that's symbolic too.

SARAH/SAM: Yes, it's symbolic. The bread and the cup at the communion table remind us of Jesus, and we eat them to remember him. We retell the story of his life, death, and resurrection and remember him with the bread and wine.

ZACK: Or grape juice!

SARAH/SAM: Right, or grape juice!

ORBITUS: Or grape juice?

ZACK: Well, originally, Jesus probably used wine, but some churches, like ours, use grape juice also, so that kids and adults who don't want to have alcohol can have something else to share. They're both made from grapes, so it's close.

ORBITUS: I'm still starved—can I have both?

ZIPZOR: *(rolls her eyes and ignores him)* So tell me, does everyone who follows Jesus participate in this communion?

SARAH/SAM: Sure. People who follow Jesus are called Christians, and Christians all over the world celebrate communion.

ZIPZOR: And everyone has this same bread and wine or grape juice?

RAELYN: Well, not exactly. Different people in different parts of the world have different kinds of bread. Some even have these special wafers made just for communion. You just use whatever bread you have in your part of the world—remember, it's symbolic.

SARAH/SAM: And some have only wine, others only grape juice, some both just like us.

ZACK: And people serve it in different ways, too. Some people break off pieces of one loaf and drink out of the same cup. Others have lots of little pieces and little cups. Some even break off the bread and dip it into the cup. It just depends.

ZIPZOR: Interesting! So you can choose to remember Jesus with the bread and cup in many different ways?

ZACK: Exactly.

ORBITUS: Well, I wanna know what happened to dinner. First you said there was dinner involved, now there's no dinner?

SARAH/SAM: With Jesus and his original followers there was a dinner. And in the early days of the church, they continued the tradition of having a dinner, but we sort of got away from that a long time ago.

ORBITUS: *(disappointed)* What a bummer.

ZACK: But you know, we do still eat together. After worship is over, and after we share the communion meal, we go next door for fellowship time where there's cookies and cake and stuff.

ORBITUS: Cookies!

RAELYN: We'd love to have you join us. You can be a part of our worship service and we'll share communion with you. Then we can all go to fellowship time together.

ZIPZOR: We'd be honored to join you. I'd really like to learn more about this Jesus person.

SARAH/SAM: Good, because that's the only requirement to come to the communion table. Anyone and everyone is welcome to share the meal, so long as they have a genuine desire to know and follow Jesus in their lives.

ZACK: So let's have a seat and share communion together.

(All sit together in the front row.)

Jennifer Mills-Knutsen and St. Luke's UCC Jeffersonville, Indiana, middle school class (2006)

11

BREATHE DEEP THE BECKONING SEA
Words for Baptism

NOW TO THE ONE WHO IS ABLE TO KEEP YOU
FROM FALLING, AND TO MAKE YOU STAND WITHOUT
BLEMISH IN THE PRESENCE OF GLORY WITH
REJOICING, TO THE ONLY GOD OUR SAVIOR
THROUGH JESUS CHRIST OUR LORD, BE GLORY,
MAJESTY, POWER, AND AUTHORITY, BEFORE ALL
TIME AND NOW AND FOREVER. AMEN.

Jude 1:25

baptize

face down, warm, lying the sun
an ant climbs quartz
washed into sea

run downstream from ancient cliff,
carried to ocean,
grain by grain

waters that birth and baptize and clean,
sea-salt encrusting,
I am received

and I on this day long simply my life
come, breathe deep
the beckoning sea.

William B. Jones

For Baptism Sundays

Holy One, are you a sink-or-swim God, or the kind that eases us into the water? We have come here today, in all species: both those aquaphobic from early hurts and betrayals, and water babies who never want to get out of the tub. Take us as we are, and shape us into the people you call us to be, disciples and followers in the good-hearted, whole-bodied Way of Jesus. Amen.

Molly Phinney Baskette

Service of Baptism

Dear ones, we are here to celebrate life—life in Christ!
At various times you will be cued by the music to join in this song. Let's learn it.

A sacrament is an outward sign of inward grace. The sacrament of baptism is both God's gift and our response to that gift. We believe that baptism places each of us into the body of Christ, the church, which is the universal church of believers in Christ, and the sacrament is big enough, strong enough, and cleansing enough to last forever.

God's love for us has no beginning and no ending. Parents, overflowing with love for their children, act on their faith in bringing their precious little ones to be baptized. They acknowledge that to raise children in faith takes a whole community, like this one. People in the congregation will be teachers, mentors, surrogate grandparents, and role models in a young person's faith journey. When children reach an age of discernment, we as a congregation will offer preparation and an opportunity for them to make their own commitment of faith, to *confirm, or make firm,* what baptism has already begun. The journey of faith is lifelong, and baptism is a sacred milestone on it.

_____ , if you are ready to continue on this journey, please bring your child, _____ , into the aisle, into the midst of this congregation, facing the font and the cross. _____ 's godparent(s), _____ may stand in support of you.

Congregation sings:
In this sacrament we embrace God's eternal grace.
We are all God's sons and daughters. Welcome in these sacred waters.

Here in this body of Christ, this congregation, we live out our faith. We rejoice in our diversity and celebrate that which we hold in unity. Please join us as we unite with the church in all times and places in affirming our faith in the triune God:

Do you believe in God?

I believe in God!

Do you believe in Jesus Christ?

I believe in Jesus Christ!

Do you believe in the Holy Spirit?

I believe in the Holy Spirit!

To parents and godparents

Look to the cross, symbol of our faith. Jesus is not there; he is risen and lives among us in the presence of the Holy Spirit. Jesus dared to welcome everyone in radical inclusivity—even children! In our journey of faith, we commit ourselves to live in love as he did, turning away from the murky waters that drag humanity down, to the crystal waters that buoy us up. Will you join us on this journey?

PARENT(s): Yes, I will, with the help of God.

Then please move forward to the baptismal font.

Congregation sings:

In this sacrament we embrace God's eternal grace.
We are all God's sons and daughters. Welcome in these sacred waters.

_____, you have already been baptized. Will you renew the commitment made for you, and continue on this challenging journey?

PARENT(s): Yes, I will, with the help of God.

Then receive the sign of the cross on your forehead in renewal of your baptism. Again, look to the cross. Because of Jesus' risks of faith, his enemies saw to it that he was put to death. By the grace of God, death did not—and does not—have the last word. But sadly, evil does exist in the world. Baptism will not protect you or those you love from evil. In baptism we are saying, "I want to turn away from evil, accept God's gift of forgiveness, and do all in my power to extend God's goodness into the world. I understand that this is a lifelong journey of faith." Will you join us on this journey?

PARENT(s): Yes, I will, with the help of God.

Then please move forward around the baptismal font.

Congregation sings:

In this sacrament we embrace God's eternal grace.
We are all God's sons and daughters. Welcome in these sacred waters.

Do you, who witness and celebrate this sacrament, promise your love, support, and care to the one about to be baptized, as [he or she] lives and grows in Christ?

We promise our love, support, and care.

We as the body of Christ are ready and eager to surround you and your child with our love and care. You as parents and godparents hold the responsibility to see that _____ is present among us so we can live out that love.

Do you promise, by the grace of God,
to be Christ's disciple,
to grow with this child in the Christian faith,
to help [him or her] to be a faithful member of the church,
and to celebrate the presence of the Holy Spirit in all of life?

PARENT(S) AND GODPARENT(S): Yes, we promise, with the help of God.

Please join me in a spirit of prayer.
Baptismal Prayer from UCC Book of Worship or other prayer

_____, when Jesus was baptized, the spirit of God was there, saying, "You are my child, my beloved, in you I am well pleased."

_____, at this very moment, and at every moment in time, God's Spirit, God's breath, is with you, for you too are a precious child of God who is loved and blessed. *(Take the child and baptize.)*

_____, you are baptized, in the name of the Father, in the name of the Son, and in the name of the Holy Spirit, One God, Mother of us all. Amen.
Let us pray together for the one baptized today:

We give you thanks, O Holy One, mother and father of all the faithful,
for this your child and for your grace present here today
in water and the Holy Spirit.
May we all be filled with joy, and receive, nurture, and befriend

_____, a new member of the body of Christ.

_____, newly baptized:
   strength for life's journey,
   courage in time of suffering,
   the joy of faith,
   the freedom of love,
   and the hope of new life;
through Jesus Christ, who makes us one. Amen.

To the baptized
Welcome to your new family in Christ!

To the parents and godparents
With your permission, I will take _____ to meet [his or her or their] new family in Christ!

Pastor takes child or children to greet congregation.

Moderator presents certificate(s) and gift(s)
You may be seated in the congregation.

Congregation sings twice
In this sacrament we embrace God's eternal grace.
We are all God's sons and daughters. Welcome in these sacred waters.

Catherine Barker, liturgy / Philip Tschopp, music

Invitation to Baptism—Emphasizing Names · Matthew 3:16–17

We cherish this story of Jesus: when all the people were baptized, and Jesus also had been baptized, heaven opened and the Holy Spirit descended upon Jesus in bodily form like a dove. And a voice came from heaven, "You are my son, the Beloved; in you I am well pleased."

We come here to share in that Belovedness, and in that wide ranging experience of being named in the Spirit, to which Jesus invites us all. Jesus himself came to be named as God's anointed one, the Christ, and to have his own name known as a mighty name for God. So may each of us, in our small way, become someone whose name brings to the minds and hearts of others a ready recognition of blessing, peace, integrity, commitment, conviction, grace, and love—things we know that come from God.

As _____ moves from the river of blessing into the wilderness of life, we pray that [his or her] name and life will show forth God's life and wisdom. Already [he or she] is fully engaged in the life of the Spirit, has known tears and laughter, joy and sorrow. With full hearts _____ and _____ seek the blessing of the Holy Spirit for their beloved child, praying their little one may be strengthened by God's grace to meet steadfastly all struggles in this life.

We mark _____ today with the water of God's abiding love, and pray that every day of this one's life [he or she] may remind [himself or herself] that [he or she] is God's own, and God and God's people are well pleased in [him or her].

Nancy Rockwell

12

LAUGHING AND BULRUSHES
Some Special Services

BUT GROW IN THE GRACE AND KNOWLEDGE
OF OUR LORD AND SAVIOR JESUS CHRIST.
TO HIM BE THE GLORY BOTH NOW AND TO
THE DAY OF ETERNITY. AMEN.

2 Peter 3:18

Opening Prayer In Celebration of Science and Technology · Genesis 1

God of All
whose Love fires the sun and spins the planets
we acknowledge you as our Creator,
Maker of the Universe
blessed and generous beyond knowing.

Made in your image,
We seek to be partners with you in creation
Through innovation and the exploration
    of ideas and technology,
Using both intellect and imagination
in our work and in our worship.

Filled with the breath of your Spirit,
We stand in awe
As discovery and insight lead us
    to better understand your world,

As vision and leadership guide us
    to live in closer harmony
with your ever evolving ecology.

God of All
We give you thanks
For invention and progress
For those who dream and dare
For divine collaboration through ethics and conscience.

And we give you thanks for minds and hearts
    with which we may question and analyze
    with which we may seek to know you
    with which we may learn to love more deeply
        this world which you have made.
Amen

Anne G. Cohen

Call to Worship for Fair Trade Worship Service

Whether your mug says
    kiss me I'm Irish,
    World's Greatest Dad
        or Granddad or Golfer
Whether it declares
    this is my drug of choice
Or warns
    I haven't had my coffee yet—
        don't make me kill you
Whether it has a smiley face or your child's baby face,
    a rainbow flag or your puppy dog,
Even if it has a Monet watercolor or
    Vincent Van Gogh's vanishing ear as you drink it,
It is unlikely that it says—
I am drinking coffee picked by the leathered
    hands of a farmer, a harvester who
    has waited years for this plant to be covered
        in its white jasmine-scented flower,

only to wait a few days more
    for the flower to cede its space
        to dark green berries,
to watch them with care as they ripen
    from yellow to deepest red and to know *the* moment
    when pulling them from the plant
        will produce that heady richness—picking them
            neither too early nor too late.
The mug will not tell of the long hours of picking the bean
    at this narrow peak of perfection
        in order to secure the best price,
it will not tell of the hot sun or rain filled days,
    of the heavy sacks or stooped backs
        or fears of a feeble harvest.
It will not tell of the tentative way of life
    that the coffee bean asks of the farmer;
but the story is there—all there in the dark liquid
    of the coffees and espressos, or in
the delicate leaves of hand-picked tea, or
    deep in the fabric of hand-sewn clothes.
And so we gather together, as we are doing now,
    to tell each other the stories of the beginnings,
    middles and ends, to pay attention,
        and think about how things can be different, and better.
To trade in a mass-produced ceramic
    World's Greatest anything,
for a small cup, fashioned by the potter's hand,
    that may have scratched in its clay, the simple words,
    trying to be God's faithful . . . .
Welcome to this hour
    where we will open a window
        to a greener land, to cleaner skies,
            to the idea of a fairer life for all
and to consider a cash crop in hope
    for a world
        that is about to turn

Abigail Hastings

Music Appreciation Sunday

Creator of the harmony of the spheres—some heavenly intuition tunes our ears to what you compose—and so we praise you beyond the limits of words.

Originator of the fugue of a billion variations—some among us have picked up the theme you've stated, captured a piece of it, put it on a page, then "pushed it through a horn, till it was born into a new psalm." Thank you for sharing so freely what is yours by holy copyright.

You father forth the good news, you are mother to the blues, you say, "Yes, children, here is your part." And so your sinners, saints, and angels jam together, and mortals take their solo riffs.

God of the dance tune, there are yet more truths and melodies to break forth from your heavenly hymnal, more rhythms, sounds, furies, and silences. More ways to sing down grace, more ways to raise praise than an eternity can hold.

Holy is your name, holy your game.

David Slater

Music Appreciation Sunday

God of many harmonies, God of different drummers, God of unity, we thank you for the gift of music! We rejoice that you invite us to come into your presence with hymns, rhythms, and instruments. When we have a song in our heart, you encourage us to make a joyful noise and fill the earth with thanksgiving! When we sit and weep and wonder how we will ever lift up our songs to you again, you invite us to join our voices in psalms of lament that help us give voice to our sorrow. And when we experience the renewal of your grace and blessings, you revel in our choruses of alleluias. Remind us, God, that there truly is a song for every season of our lives. You dwell with us in those seasons and promise to hear our prayers, whether spoken, sung, or silent. Amen.

Kathryn J. Campbell

How Do You See God? Making a Hymn Come Alive

(Using "Bring Many Names" by Brian Wren)

Sing "Bring Many Names" (verses one and two)
Santina, a young mother:

I am a mother. In fact, I am a mother of three very energetic boys. I'm up early each day, preparing lunches, making lists, planning the day, getting two of them to school. I multitask. I laugh. I cry. I worry. I have to get to work and sometimes must do so with my little guy hanging on my leg. I am blessed and I am exhausted. I see God best as a strong mother, like me.

Sing verse three
Bob, a young father:

I am a father. I go to work each day and wonder, "What am I missing? How are the kids doing in school?" When I'm home, I'm completely theirs, but my life is torn between work—which involves long hours and travel—and home, which demands both play and discipline. I wonder what the kids will be like when they grow up. I wonder what it will be like to spend some time alone again with my partner. I think God wonders too. I see God best as a caring father, like me.

Sing verse four
Joe, an elderly retired minister:

I am old—well, not that old—but I've been around for a while. Like the old skin horse in the Velveteen Rabbit, I've got some aching, worn out joints, and most of my hair has been rubbed off. But I'm real. I have more time now to give and receive love. I also have more time to think about life—the life I've lived and the lives of those I love. I have time to pray—sometimes with great joy and sometimes with a broken heart. I think that's the way God feels about us as well. I see God best as seasoned and experienced, like me.

Sing verse five
Mitchell, an adolescent:

I am a teenager. I am young. I've got things to do, places to go, people to see. I've got homework to finish and friends to meet. Have you seen that movie? Can you come to my party? I'm not always sure about God. At times I'm not even sure God exists, but if God does, I bet God looks a lot like me.

Sing verse six

Scott Landis

BRIGHT SUNDAY OR HOLY HUMOR SUNDAY

We join with God in laughing at death's hold on us. The service is traditionally the Sunday after Easter and the worship order is turned upside down just as our world was with the resurrection. Surprises abound as they did for the disciples on the first Easter morning . . . the unexpected becomes the playful norm. Balloons, bubbles, butterflies, and clowns have appeared over the years.

Reverse the Worship Service Rubrics!

Blessed are they who laugh at themselves, for they shall never cease to be amused.

Fellowship Time "Knock-knock"

Scatter knock knock jokes throughout the service. Salt the bulletins with them. (Singing, Greetings and Announcements)

Postlude: Take It Away, Key Duster

Benediction

1: Listen to God's breath within, it is fluttering over our belief

MANY: We are happy resurrection people.

UNO: The world is upside down now: the Spirit has pushed its way through.

MANY : We are joyful resurrection people.

UN: The world is upside down now: death's despair has been replaced with joy!

MANY : We are hilarious resurrection people.

ONE: The world is upside down now: we can say with conviction, our God is an awesome God!

MANY : We are light-hearted and ecstatic resurrection people. Let's celebrate God!

Second Reading · Psalm 67

First Reading · Isaiah 40:27–31

Doxology

Praise God from whom our humor flows
Praise God all joyful hearts below
Praise Spirit with whom our hearts soar
Praise Christ whose smile is evermore

Dedication Prayer

We've heard, O God, that you love a cheerful giver, so we offer you our life with joy. We sense that you are sending us, as Jesus was sent, to share joy with the world. We dedicate our time, talents, and skills as jesters to continue spreading the good news to this depressed world. May your creative playfulness bubble up in surprising ways through us. Amen.

Called to Worship in the World

1: Go! Taking your doubts, your hopes, and your faith

A FEW: Christ is risen! Yipee!

1: Go! In spite of your questions, your wonderings, and your misgivings

MORE: Christ is risen! Hooray!

1: Go! Overcoming your fear, your sadness, and your timidness.

A LOT: Christ is risen! Yeehaw!

1: Go! Rejoicing and worshiping God, the One who lifts us from death to new life.

EVERYBODY: Christ is risen, you betcha! Our faith takes off! Amen.

Prelude: Here's Key Duster!

Susan Hamilton

~

WOMEN AT THE WATER: A WORSHIP OUTLINE · Exodus 1:8–2:10

Preparation for Congregational Worship

Decorate the communion table in a "Nile" river motif with blue, silver, or gray fabrics. Drape the fabric so it flows off the table onto the floor. Place rocks at the base of the table and include plants. Stuffed exotic animals or a small portable water foun-

tain will create a multisensory experience. Use woven baskets as offering plates. When entering the sanctuary, children can be given small cut-out fish to place anywhere on the "river" before the service starts. During the Call to Worship, the leader might either stand at the baptismal font or place a bowl of water on the communion table, dipping his or her hand in the water and pouring some out at each refrain.

Call to Worship

Come to the water and remember!

We remember the life-giving waters of our mothers' wombs.

Come to the water and remember!

We remember God's spirit brooding like a mother-hen over the face of the primordial waters.

Come to the water and remember!

We remember how God birthed life anew after the flood-waters.

Come to the water and remember!

Women at the water saved Moses; God's power allowed Moses to part the water and save the multitude. God's mercy and justice rushes out like a mighty stream. We remember and praise God!

Confession · Exodus 1:8–14

God of all people, we confess that have not loved our neighbors as ourselves.
Even more so, we have oppressed and alienated them.
Like Pharaoh who did not know Joseph or his people,
we have failed to take the time to get to know our neighbors.
Like the Egyptian taskmasters who ruthlessly imposed labor,
we refuse social responsibility and accountability because we benefit economically.
Like the Egyptian people who feared the ancient Israelites,
we, too, let fear instill values of exploitation and hatred against our neighbors.
Allow us, O God, to hear once again the stories of the underrepresented, the marginalized, and the oppressed.
Teach us, O God, how we might delight in life instead of ignoring the miseries of our neighbors.

Assurance of Grace

Hear the good news! God is faithful and just, slow to anger, and abounding in forgiveness. God's mercy, evident through the actions of the women whose stories we will hear today, pours out for all people!

Scripted Reading · Exodus 1:15–22

Two women in costumes represent Hebrew midwives Shiphrah and Puah.

SHIPHRAH: I can't do it. I just can't.

PUAH: Shiphrah, we are nothing to nobody. Pharaoh has the power. We have to do what he says or we will die.

SHIPHRAH: No, Puah, God has power over life and death, not Pharaoh.

PUAH: God? Where is our God? Too long have our people cried out to God in the midst of suffering and enslavement. God has done nothing to save our people.

SHIPHRAH: Puah, don't say that. It is Pharaoh who has enslaved us, not God.

PUAH: But where will God be when I hold each new, little, Hebrew baby boy in my arms? We must face a decision whether or not to slaughter the innocent after we withdraw them from their mothers' wombs. No one should have to make that decision.

SHIPHRAH: So we lie to Pharaoh.

PUAH: We lie?

SHIPHRAH: We are Hebrew women midwives. Like God, we preserve life. Where is God, Puah? God is in our decision to lie in the face of oppression; to save our people and uphold the sanctity of all the lives of God's children, no matter what their race or ethnicity.

Pause. Two other women rush in, one Moses' mother, Jochebed, and the other Moses' sister, Miriam. Jochebed is holding a baby-doll wrapped in a blanket.

JOCHEBED: You have to help me, Shiphrah and Puah. I can't let Pharaoh's people throw my child into the Nile! I can no longer hide him but if I keep him he will die! No mother should ever have to make this decision.

PUAH: *(looking around and finding a basket)* Here—we will put him in this basket and seal it so it will float.

SHIPHRAH: We will have to take a chance on the waters. His watery death-sentence might actually be his saving grace!

The women sit in the front and add "pitch" to the bottom of the basket, each having a small role of masking tape and tearing off one-inch strips to overlap on one another. (Or invite children or other congregants to help them during musical interlude.)

Musical Interlude

(Suggestions include an instrumental or vocal soloist, choir anthem, liturgical dancers bringing in strips of fabric, rocks, or plants to add to the "river.")

Reading Continues . . .   ·   Exodus 2:1–10

Jochebed places the baby in a basket and sets the basket on the floor. Shiphrah, Puah, and Jochebed exit. Miriam remains a slight distance behind and watches. Pharaoh's daughter enters in royal attire.

MIRIAM: *(Addressing congregation)* I've seen her before in royal pomp and circumstance. That is Pharaoh's daughter! She is a person of privilege and wealth; she is an Egyptian. Certainly she will see my baby brother and tell her father!

PHARAOH'S DAUGHTER: *(Retrieving the basket)* This must be one of the Hebrews' children! What a beautiful child! What am I to do with you? If the waters of the Nile have not drowned you, then certainly my father's people will! How can the life of one little child cause such fear among my people? No one should have to make the decision whether or not to lead such a child to death. Though the rules of my society tell me not to, I will save you! *(Miriam, overhearing, approaches Pharaoh's daughter.)*

MIRIAM: Your Royal Highness, I know of a Hebrew woman who could take care of that child for you.

PHARAOH'S DAUGHTER: Go and get her.

(Miriam runs out and comes back with Jochebed. Pharaoh's daughter addresses her.)

Take this child and nurse it for me, and I will give you your wages.

(Pharaoh's daughter hands the baby to Jochebed. She and Miriam exit.)

I will name the child Moses. I drew him out of the water and saved his life. In the same way, God has drawn me to the water to save my own life. God has shown me a way to stop a cycle of oppression and exploitation in my own society. I have a feeling God will continue to perform life-saving acts for all people! *(Exit)*

Closing Prayer

We thank you, O God, for showing us acts of mercy through the women at the water. We celebrate strength and courage like that of Shiphrah and Puah, which allowed them to defy unjust orders. Give all of us some portion of the love Jochebed had for her child that helped her to remain faithful to the preservation of life. As Pharaoh's daughter dedicated herself to ending patterns of oppression and exploitation, we ask that you too constantly remind us of ways in which we can build a world wherein the sanctity of life remains paramount to our existence. Show us how we can work towards your vision of justice and mercy for all people. We pray this in the name of Jesus Christ, Amen.

Katherine Low

A Liturgy for Leaving

LEADER: The journey of life offers us many opportunities to live in various communities as we earn our living, raise families, recover and heal, or retire. Sometimes the unknown of an impending move fosters feelings of anxiety and sometimes of embarking on an exciting adventure. Whenever we leave one location for another, we value words of supportive encouragement from our friends and family. Today, we will offer such support to _____ as s/he prepare to move from here to a new home in _____. I invite _____ to come forward at this time.

_____ , receive our appreciation of you and prayers for your new life. You have offered freely your time and talents for the work of Christ through this church. You have shared with us your loving, generous, and playful spirit.

We have worked with you and laughed with you. We shall miss your open hearts, your smiles, and your creative ideas.

The inviting nature you possess reflects the hospitality of Abraham and Sarah. Many have felt welcome in your home and at our church because of your kindness.

We give thanks for your faithful service to God while with us and we celebrate with your new community as they receive you into their lives and ministry.

The memories of our time together will be honored as a treasured part of the history of our church. May your memories of our love support you in your Christian walk even in the uncertain transitional times

Do not worry about anything, but in everything by prayer and supplication with thanksgiving let your requests be made known to God (Philippians 4:6).

PERSON WHO IS LEAVING: We/I will take the love and blessings of this church with us/me, remembering to do good to one another, be joyful always, pray at all times, and be thankful in all circumstances.

LEADEr: And now that your time with us has ended, go and begin your new journey, guided by God's love and this prayer: May the God of Sarah and Abraham, who watches over all the families of the earth, bless you as you establish your new home in peace and steadfast love.

May God bless you and keep you. May God's face shine upon you and be gracious to you. May God look upon you with kindness and give you peace. Amen. (Numbers 6:24–25)

Susan Hamilton

13

UNDER OUR ROOF

Liturgy For Homes, Marriage, and Companion Animals

RESTORE TO THEM, THIS VERY DAY,
THEIR FIELDS, THEIR VINEYARDS, THEIR
OLIVE ORCHARDS AND THEIR HOUSES. . . .
AND ALL THE ASSEMBLY SAID, "AMEN,"
AND PRAISED GOD. AND THE PEOPLE DID
AS THEY HAD PROMISED."

Nehemiah 5:11a, 13b

HOUSE BLESSING

Words at the Front Door

A parable from the desert fathers has one monk exclaim that he wishes to "when alone, be as open and lighthearted as he is when with others, when with others, be as honest and humble as I am when alone." Bless this doorway, God, bless the going out and coming in of all who gather here. May strangers be as old friends to *(family name(s))*, and may they be blessed to entertain the occasional angel unawares.

Words at the Kitchen Table

May this table stand as a symbol for the whole house. As the place where children may sit and be fed by their parents, and eventually learn to eat themselves, make it a place of love. As the place where *(names of family members)* will both remember old times and plan for their future, sharing a cup of tea at the end of the day, make it a place of peace. As the place where diverse groups of people may gather and be one, where piles of the ordinary stuff of life—receipts, letters, to-do lists, and love notes—may accumulate, bless everything they stand for: the sharing of good news and bad news, responsibilities and freedoms, prosperous times and lean times.

Inscense

Light and "smudge" each room in turn with frankincense, which aroma'd Christ's first home. God, grant that each room in this house be put to its own proper use. May the bedrooms grant this family refreshment, peace, and intimacy. May the living room grant them safe space to be a family alone, in community with one another, and in privacy, when they wish it, from extended family and friends. May the bathrooms be a place of nurture, self-care, and healthfulness, and the dining room a place of conviviality and generosity. Banish any residual energy from previous occupants from this space, and free it to be filled to overflowing with the life you have promised in abundance to *(names of family members)*, and to the generations that will follow them. As this smoke rises, may our prayers rise to you.

Baptism

To family: You already bless this house by your presence, by your warmth, by your laughter, by your years of friendship past and years promised in the future. I invite you now to add a further blessing to this home by sprinkling it with this branch dipped in a little water—the water is from *(name a local body of water, and what history it may have for the forebears of the family, and a branch from any local connection)*. Both together baptize this house with new life.

Gifts

Furthermore, we offer you these gifts:
Bread: that this house might never know hunger
Salt: that life in this house might always have flavor
Wine: that joy and prosperity may reign here forever

Benediction

As Christ honored so many houses with his presence, from the humble hut to the rich palace, may he honor yours today! Amen.

Have everybody bang some pots and pans for joy!

Molly Phinney Baskette

HOUSE BLESSING SERVICE

A small table in the center of the circle of family and friends serves as an "altar" on which a candle is lit, a small flowering plant and the blessing water within a chalice is placed.

Opening Words · Ephesians 2:19–22

ONE: No one can build a home with any greater material than the love and grace of God.

ALL: Our home is built on the foundation of Christ,

ONE: Who stands as the doorway to a holy and sacred life,

ALL: And in whom we are being built together to become a dwelling in which the Spirit of God lives.

ONE: So then, we are no longer foreigners and strangers,

FRIENDS: But citizens with the saints,

FAMILY: And also members of God's household;

ONE: Built on the foundation of the apostles and prophets,

ALL: With Christ as the chief cornerstone.

Blessing of the Home, Room by Room

ONE: May this home be a place of rest, renewal and refreshment for the _____ family.

FRIENDS: May the light of Christ always shine in this home.

FAMILY: May God's Spirit and word be a guide for our daily lives.

ONE: May God's Spirit bless this home and may God's guarding angels protect and watch over you.

FAMILY: Bless us, O God, that we may find here shelter, peace, and health. Make our house a haven for all who enter it and may all guests be received as if they were Christ.

FRIENDS: God will keep your going out and your coming in from this time on and forevermore.

ALL: Amen.

Susan Hamilton

HOUSE START UP CEREMONY—HABITAT FOR HUMANITY

People's response is "You have been building here for a long time."

Eternal God, by your Breath, your Word, and your Potter's Hands, you evolved this land from mud and light. In the fullness of time you baptized this holy land in the waters of the sea. At your call, the earth beneath shook, as the hills pushed the rocks from the hot depths of the earth to the cool surface. With your mighty breath you swept the waters to the west and to the south to reveal our desert paradise and this lot of land. It pleased you, O God, that the earth brought forth cactus and succulents found nowhere else on planet earth—Saguaro, Cholla, and Penstamen—while rabbits danced and lizards basked, while cactus wren and desert mouse watched warily for red-tail hawk and diamondback. And all knew they were on sacred ground together. Loving God,

You have been building here for a long time.

We thank you that again you blessed this land, as the feet of the ancestors, made in your own image, traversed this land each year far to the north and south, as you called them to follow their crops and herds by seasons of planting and harvest, for shearing and spinning, Holy people in your image who walked and lived and multiplied upon this land—knowing it belonged to you. Loving God,

You have been building here for a long time.

You hallowed this land by your One Spirit in both the old world missionary traveler and the new world migrant and tenant and blessed them both with learning from one another—and as they spoke together of the day you hallowed all earth by dwelling among us in Jesus as one of us, in a desert land like ours, living, dying and rising to bring your creation and all of us to new life. Loving God,

You have been building here for a long time.

We thank you, Holy God, for your Spirit in the hearts of all the people who ever lived here and for your Spirit in the people of your church and of Habitat for Humanity, and for your Spirit in the *(names of family members)*, as all together—all these your people have built this beautiful home with the strength, skill, and love you gave them. Loving God,

You have been building here for a long time.

Continue to bless, O God, the *(family name(s))* as they share life in this home they have dreamed of, and as they share life with their new neighbors and as they help to make this a community of love and justice and friendship. Teach us faith and love and hope as we witness your Spirit in their grace and their love for one another—and in their deep gratitude for your holy hands, O God, in the hands of these your people who have worked and built this house together. Bless the builders and the congregations of your people that they represent. Bless those who donated time and materials and money and love. Loving God,

You have been building here for a long time.

Holy Trinity, God above us, God beside us, God within and among us, you have been building here for a long time. Now, we ask that you bless this house, the work of your love through our hands and bless all these your people with that sense of Holy Satisfaction you grant when we have done what you asked us to do. We pray in the name of the Father, and of the Son, and of the Holy Spirit. Amen.

Stephen E. Wayles

A Prayer and House Blessing

Bless this house, O God, we pray. Keep it safe by night and day, safe from destruction of storm or unrest, safe from the winds of outrageous fortune. May this house be shelter, a resting place. May it be built on a sure foundation: faith in God and the assurance of salvation. May this be a place where Christ rules and where God is served.

Make this house a home. May this be a place where love grows, where everyone knows he or she is loved and can love with abandon. Let this be a place where respect is the way of relating, where kindness and consideration are usual. Let it be a place where people can grow and learn. May it be a place for launching people into the world, and a place that welcomes them back.

Bless the people living here. Let this be a place where people can try new things and not be defeated with teasing, or destroyed with laughter at them. May laughter with and not at anyone fill this space. Let it be a place where ideas are born and creativity nurtured. May encouragement nurture each person here. Let it be alright to explore and not be mocked.

May trust fill this space so people can be intimate, close, open, and vulnerable with one another without fear. May this house be safe from fear of unchecked anger, outbursts of rage, physical, psychological, or spiritual abuse. May discipline be merciful, the kind that leads to self-discipline. May the people here know they belong, are accepted, wanted, and appreciated.

Bless this house with wisdom. Let this be a place where people are valued: seen and accepted for who they are now, and not what they were in the past. Let this be a place where people are forgiven, truly forgiven, and failures remembered no more.

Let gratitude be expressed in abundance. May joy be overflowing. May this be a home where people really listen, and people know they are heard. May understanding be real in this home. May this be a home where feelings can be shared without recrimination, where truth is spoken with love, where your name, God, is praised and life celebrated. May this home be a place of contentment.

Bless this house, God above, with joy, contentment, warmth, and love. Bless the doors that open wide and let each welcome one inside. Bless the windows, paths for light and for viewing the world, people, places, sun, and stars. Bless each room and guard each wall. And let your peace be over all.

Elizabeth B. Congdon

Call to Wedding Celebration

for thousands of years
people have gathered
under a grove of trees
or an expanse of sky
beside an altar of marble
or beneath a cloth of blessing
to bear witness to such
a beautifully simple act
of intention and promise

for thousands of years
people have looked on
as those they love
make known their choice,

this choosing of love
and life and future

for thousands of years
people have risked
the catch in their throats
the quickening heart
the dampening eyes
to sense the pivot of a moment

where all that has come before
yields to the possibilities ahead:
the deeper trails yet to hike;
moist dark earth turning
for new vegetable seeds;
the pleasure of tossing the dinner salad
greens; or teaching new tricks
to an eager-to-learn and
uncommonly happy dog

and for us, for those of us gathered
here, as vivid to us now as this
time is, when the fullness of each
becomes the splendor of the together,
the lives we here witness and celebrate
are most piercingly imprinted
in the record of our joys
by the way they look at each other
by the light that fills that fleeting
but luxurious exchange
from the depths of one's being

it is that look, and that compass
of knowing and being
known, of loving and being loved,
that illumines all that we hope for
in this day and in the days to come.

Welcome to this celebration
of two people
of two people finding

and of us, lucky us, finding ourselves
here in the privilege
of finding ourselves in the midst of
the best that life has to offer.
the very best of what life has to offer.
Welcome, one and all, to the celebration.

Abigail Hastings

Pastoral Prayer for a Second Marriage

O God of us all, who creates and sustains the world with love,
we praise you for your faithful, loving presence, everywhere and always.
We are thankful for the event that brings us together today.

The wedding of _____ and _____ is cause for great rejoicing
in this family and this community.
We are grateful that they have chosen to commit themselves
and their marriage to you so that they might experience your guiding hand
entwined with their own as they walk this path together.

Help them to find in each other the grace and compassion
that we experience in you.
Help them to offer each other the humble, unwavering love
as witnessed in your Son, Jesus Christ.
Help them be for each other a source of strength and encouragement
as received from your Holy Spirit.
Remove from their hearts the specter of what has been,
so that they can be open to the beauty of what will be.
Gift them with courage, integrity, patience, and wisdom
so that they will not fear the challenges of their shared life,
but instead be ready to face them together.
Surround them with a caring, respectful community
that will support this couple
with their prayers, their fellowship, and their trust.

On behalf of _____ and _____, we ask all of these things
in the name of the One whose love is our past, our present, and our future,
Amen.

Susan E. Brown

Prayer After Divorce, Moving, Changing Churches
Matt. 9:20–22; Mark 5:24–34; Luke 8:42b–48

Gracious God,
It is in remembering that I see your hand.
It is in remembering sadness that I see I was not alone
But was held by you,
In tears shared, in hands held in prayer
And I touched your hem . . .

In leaving, I learned of loss, but you did not let me lose you.
At times, when I felt I was losing my way, you called my name and drew me
back with cords of love . . . a kind word, a call, a note.
And I touched your hem . . .

In the ending of a marriage you carried me through. You walked with me,
giving me others who had made the journey before me, who shared their
pain and accompanied me. You taught me to be free of resentment; you
taught me how to forgive.
And I touched your hem . . .

The darkness gradually became light, within and without, reminding me of
Peter's words to "pay attention to you, to your Word, as to a light shining in
a dark place, until the day dawns and the morning star rises in my heart." You
blessed me with a new place, a new home.
And I touched your hem . . .

You provided. You did not leave me alone to help children through their college years. When I felt the challenges and worries were too much to bear, you
gave me strength.
And I touched your hem . . .

You gave me courage in changing churches, ever reminding me that I am a
part of the body of Christ in the world, shaped by all who have gone before
me, who are with me now and who are yet to come.
And I touched your hem . . .

May I look forward with trust, with discernment, not forgetting what is behind but moving toward what lies ahead in the name of Jesus Christ. My
heart is grateful, my spirit is willing, for I have touched your hem. Amen.

Sue Henley

Wedding Resource

Blessing God, you, whose caring hands painted the natural landscape around us—the green of the trees, the blue of the mountains and the rainbow hues of the flowers; you, who created the heat of the summer day and the cool of the mountain stream; and you, who gives life to hawks and horses, cats and caterpillars:

We celebrate your love for creation and its creatures and Earth's abundant beauty. Reach out your hand in blessing on our world this morning.

Blessing God, you whose caring hands gathered us today—old and young, gay and straight, single and coupled—you who brought us safely here, from nearby and from far away:

We celebrate the gathering of our diverse body and our love for one another. Reach out your hand in blessing on our community this morning.

Blessing God, you whose caring hands fashioned us from seed and egg within our mother's womb, you who know our every strength and frailty and our daily needs and desires:

We celebrate your intimate love for us and our never-ending relationship with you. Reach out your hand in blessing on us this morning.

And by the blessing of your hand encourage and empower us to become

caretakers for creation, caregivers to community, and ever closer to you, our Creator.

Noël Nickle

BLESSING OF THE ANIMALS

This is a wonderful opportunity for intergenerational, interactive worship. For the animals' sake, this service is best outdoors, which places limits on music/ microphones, and the like, but allows all kinds of animals to come. I ask that animals either be in a carrier or cage or on a leash/reins. October 4 is St. Francis of Assisi's Feast Day. Christian Education Sunday or Earth Day or any summer Sunday are also appropriate.

Call to Worship (based on Psalm 148)

Praise God!

Praise God from the heavens. Praise God to the heights!

Praise God, all you angels!

Praise God, sun and moon and all you shining stars!

ALL: Let everyone and everything praise God's name.
For God commanded and they were created.

Praise God from the earth, you sea monsters and all deeps,

fire and hail, snow and frost, stormy wind,

mountains and all hills, fruit trees and all cedars,

beasts and all cattle, creeping things and flying birds

ALL: Let everything praise God's name! Praise God!

Time of Confession (in unison)

God of All Being,
Too often we look at the universe as if it were a collection of objects instead of the miracle of your spirit incarnating. We do not recognize other creatures as wonders of your unfolding love, do not see the robin as our brother or the tiger as our sister. We have failed to honor air, earth, and water as aspects of your being and true habitat of all animals. God, replace both our pride and our shame with true humility. Restore us to the astonishment of having a rightful place in the family of your cosmos. Amen.

Assurance of Pardon

The spirit of Love created this world of breathtaking variety with intrinsic interdependence. Humans were created to be the living mirror of nature, reflective participants in this web of life. God has blessed us with the capacity to hope and to imagine our relationship with other animals and the elements of earth. We can find our place in the community of God's creation. If we truly repent and change our wasteful ways, we can be forgiven.

Offertory

The church may wish to have the offering go toward a local animal shelter, an animal rescue team, or a Heifer purchase—any offering that particularly focuses an awareness of animals as a kind of "neighbor" we are to love or how animals participate in the healing of the world.

Prayer of Dedication

All life comes from you, O God, the air around us and our ability to breathe. Our financial well-being and our ability to earn it. All life is a gift. Let us take our place in the circle, taking what we need with one hand, passing on what another needs with the other. Amen.

Hymn

Depending on your congregation and/or the mood of your service, you may want to stay with traditional hymns. A playful song, singable by even very young attendees, is "Wise Creator Made the World" sung to the tune of "Old MacDonald Had a Farm." Like the familiar children's song, name an animal and create a sound or a characteristic gesture. Examples: duck—quack; snake—hiss; lion—roar; gorilla—scratching self; bird—wings flapping.

Wise Creator made the world. This I'm blessed I know.
And for the world, God made some *(name animal)*. This I'm blessed I know.
With a _____ , _____ here and a _____ , _____ there. Here a _____ , there a _____ ,
Everywhere a _____ , _____ .
Wise Creator made the world. This I'm blessed I know.
Last verse
Wise Creator made the world. This I'm blessed I know.
And for this world, we all give thanks. This we're blessed to know.
With a thank, thank here and a thank thank there. Here a thanks, there a thanks,
Everywhere a thank, thanks,
Wise Creator made the world. This I'm blessed I know.

Prayers of the People for the Animals

Creator of us all, today we would remember those animals who have helped us become better persons by their love, animals for whom we have concern, animals who need our prayers. We would remember . . .

Persons are invited to call out the names of animals for whom they have concerns (ill or dying or endangered) and those they have loved in their lives (pets past or present.)

Blessing of the Animals

If the group is small (or there are large animals), having the animals in a circle is easiest. For larger groups, the ones who bring animals line up. The pastor asks the name of the animal, as s/he places her/his hand on the animal/cage. I say something like the following: "Carrot, thank you for loving Ellie and teaching her how to be loving to you. You are a creature of God, blessed from before you were born. Amen."

Benediction

Meister Eckhart says, "Every creature is a word of God." Listen to the God-filled word your animal is saying. Patience. Love. Peace. Joy. Take your "word" home and remember, you are a word of God too. Amen.

Priscilla L. Denham

Confession

Forgive me, O God, the sins that dog my days.
I've chewed on the bones of grudges, and buried them so I could dig them up again. I've chased my own tail in meetings, and tucked it under to run from real challenges. I've sniffed distrustfully at the vulnerable places of others, growled at strangers, barked at those dearest to me. I've played the game and caught the truth, then refused to let it out of my teeth. I've tried to deny that my very nature is to be loving and faithful.
Forgive me, God—I love and do not love your leash.
Amen.

Assurance of Grace · Mark 7:24–30

Even the dogs under the table . . .
O God, thank you for your healing and your grace.

Maren C. Tirabassi

Dedication of an Assist Dog

We welcome you, *(dog's name)*.

We give thanks to God for your gentle yet determined personality.

We trust you to assist *(name of dog's partner)*.

We are grateful for this gift to [her/him] from a caring, sustaining Creator. We appreciate your training and your passion already to follow your life work.

We speak for you, witnessing your desire to be a good assist dog.

Woof. *(That is, I will do my best.)*

We remember your still-a-puppy-desire to play this important first year of training with *(name of dog's partner)*.

We understand if you forget or let others distract you from your work.

We promise to look all we want but will try our best not to touch you or call to you when you are wearing your harness.

We dedicate you, *(dog's name)* as an Assist Dog—who, much to your joy, will give your life to guide *(name of dog's partner)* in this community and around the world.

ALL: Thanks be to God for partners who help each other, and for all who help make our journey easier. Amen.

Dallas A. (Dee) Brauninger in honor of her three leader dogs—Dolley, Treasure, and Bear.

Prayer after the Death of a Pet

Creating God, it is you who blesses the creatures, critters, and creepy-crawling, swimming, and flying ones—hamsters and bunny rabbits, dogs and cats, puppies and kittens, millipedes and centipedes, snakes and tortoises, fish and birds, fireflies and caterpillars. May they teach us lessons of loving unconditionally and receiving love unconditionally, whether for an afternoon of gentle, loving playground play or for many seasons of living in a home. And when pets die, help their companions to mark the passing with care—walking hand-in-hand away from veterinary offices or digging graves in backyards together. Bless all animal caregivers and surround them with your love in the memory of their beloved pets. Amen.

Elizabeth D. Barnum

Prayers for the Animals

Blessed God, in your wild and loving imagination you have fashioned animals of all kinds. You have given some a temperament to live at ease in our homes. Teach us what caring for them means for creation.
Help us to see that when we are inhumane to animals we dehumanize ourselves. And when we care with intelligence we participate with you in the ongoing work of creation. You have called us to care for them all, to conserve their natural environments and protect their freedoms.

Creator, we praise you
for cats and dogs, rabbits and hamsters, gerbils and turtles,
for snakes and mice and goats, for cows and pigs and llamas and buffalo,
for parakeets and parrots and lions and tigers and bears, Oh my!
For horses and donkeys and dromedaries,
for fish and dolphins and whales,
for all that has life and breath, we give you thanks.

For all who in their natural beauty amaze us, for all who in their untamed fierceness terrify us, for all who slither, for those who come out at night, for bats and skunks, for those who do their best to feast on our gardens, we praise you.

For all who in their vulnerability need us, we ask your help. And we call you as Witness to our promise to care. Help us, we pray, that the animals might call us blessed. We pray in your holy name. Amen.

David Slater

14

UNDER OUR STEEPLE

Liturgy for the Community of Faith
with a Section on Stewardship

Whoever speaks must do so as one
speaking the very words of God; whoever
serves must do so with the strength that
God supplies, so that God may be glorified
in all things through Jesus Christ.
To him belongs the glory and the power
forever and ever. Amen.

1 Peter 4:11

Prayer before Choir Practice

Great Singer, let our songs be as prayers and our prayers be as song. Lift our voices in common witness to your love and your gospel. Let us be patient as we practice together—patient with ourselves, patient with each other, and patient with the work of your Holy Spirit. Let us take the time and effort we need to be a worthy community of voices giving glory to your name. Amen.

Sheryl Stewart

Psalm/Litany for a New Day; Installation, Church Anniversary, Renewal of Covenant · Psalm 104, Psalm 46:10, Revelation 21:23

For mountains, plains and gardens
    praise our God.
For hawk and crane and robin
    praise our God.

For sun and shadow, trees and river,
    deer and trout and squirrel,
For life and breath and song,
    praise our God.

In ringing praise and silence—
    you are there.
In deep debate we listen—
    you are there.
In laughter, dark night, hugs and handshakes,
    word and bread and study
In work and hope and Christ
    you are there.

Toward vision hid in mist
    lead us on.
Toward healing of the children
    lead us on.
Till all's forgiven, bread abounds,
    and we embrace love's hand,
Till sun and moon are gone
    lead us on.

Kathryn J. Campbell

A Prayer for a Pulpit Search Committee

Almighty God, what an awesome task we have! You have called our church into being. You have called the men and women whose profiles are sent for us to review. It awes us to propose only one candidate to lead us when it is our God who has called each applicant into ministry.

Jesus, whose gospel will be taught by the words and example of the one whom we call, we do not dare have the arrogance to do this without prayer. Nor do we think that our task of prayer for the ministry of our community will end with the installation of whomever will be our new pastor.

Holy Spirit, grant us honesty that we may present the strengths and weaknesses of our community clearly to those who come as candidates here. Grant that our vision of the needs and present mission of our church be in tune with the design you have for us in this time and place. Grant us the gift of discernment that we may know the one who will not only lead us but have the humility to learn and grow with us in faith.

Finally, dear God, remind us that your Son is already here. Let us not place the burden of Christ's perfection on any man or woman. We are all fallible sinners, saved by grace. Our leader is our shepherd, but she or he is also a lamb, just like us. Grant our leader grace to lead, but also grace to walk beside us as, together, we follow the Great Shepherd, Jesus, in whose name we pray. Amen.

Sheryl Stewart

Church Meetings

We open church meetings with a prayer. But our leaders, aware that the Holy Spirit might need some help when it comes to church politics, ask for no secret paper ballots, which might spoil our efforts at unity. To help the Dove take flight we feather it with facts as we are pleased to find them, and when opposing logic shoots it down, we fluff its wings and try to keep it aloft with testimonials. If the Flame begins to fade we heat it up with holy hectoring—take personal umbrage, tear up, question motives. If opinion shifts we always know that in our parliamentary procedure is a Wind we can direct. If in the end inconvenient questions remain we bury them with shovels full of words—being as we are cronies of chronos. And when through exhaustion and intimidation we get the bird to perch, the fire to die, the wind to cease, and most of the hands raised, our leaders clap and make the whole group sing, "Praise God from Whom All Blessings Flow."

David Slater

A Prayer Beginning a Craft Guild Session

God of Heaven and Earth, the Holy Spirit was sent in ages past to inspire the artisans and teachers of all kinds of crafts to create beauty to glorify you. What is made to the glory of God is like a sermon that reveals your will, an anthem that magnifies your glory, or the wise words of a prophet or teacher leading us into your very presence.

Creating, crafting, busy God, made in your divine image, we must create as well. Help us learn and share the skills we aspire to use to apply a love of doing and making, given to us by your own Spirit. May we carry on ancient, endangered crafts so that they may not die out. May we develop new skills and new mediums to grace, in every way, the community of faith.

Whatever we make, great or small, may it function as a prayer. It may be porcupine quill work, counted cross-stitch, quilting, or just fuzzy pompons with wiggle eyes glued on. Our crafts may grace a sanctuary or a baby's cradle, hang from a Christmas tree or a doorknob, stay in our home, or go to the ends of the earth. In every case, may what we make reflect your love, dear God, our Savior. So may it ever be, Amen.

Sheryl Stewart

Prayer before a Church Potluck

Feasting God, we gather this evening as a community of faith connected to one another through the work and love of this church. May our bodies be nourished by the foods prepared in kitchens miles apart from one another yet gathered together at this table for our evening's meal. May we digest the richness of the variety of tastes and textures before us. And may our conversations be full of curiosity and delight. As we stand with a potpourri of choices spread before us, may we serve one another in gratitude. Thanks be to God. Amen.

Elizabeth D. Barnum

Prayer before Choir Practice

Loving Creator of our voices, you have inspired the compositions of great anthems and humble choruses. You direct the choirs of angels and the music of the spheres. Yet, you are also the origin and audience for the countless songs of every bird and beast and you are the lullaby trembling in the wind amid the grasses of all the meadows. You have crafted each of our voices and called us together tonight with a desire to please you, praise you, and to share the gift of music with you, among ourselves, and in preparation for our testimony before our family of faith.

Lift our hearts and minds as well as our vocal cords, so that we may be able to express the glory that has touched us in your gospel. Open the hearts, spirits, and minds of those who listen, as well as their ears, that your message would resound for them. Though silent, may the congregation sing with us in their hearts.

Bless *(name of musician/choir director)* as [he/she] plays the music, directs, and refines us. Grant that we may provide *(name of pastor)*, our pastor, with a fitting background for [his/her] sermon and an enabling chord that might open up the entire worship experience. Be also with those of us who cannot be here to practice tonight. May all the hopes of this prayer be true for them if they are able to join us this Sunday, and may any difficulties in their health, lives, or schedules be soon eased.

Finally, blend us in harmony that we may not be a collection of solos but a true choir community of one voice for your glory. In Jesus' name, Amen.

Sheryl Stewart

Prayer for a Women's Retreat

Generous God, Source of all good gifts,
We give thanks for this time, this place,
with you and with one another.

You have called each of us by name.
You draw us to you with cords of love.
We have heard your voice saying,
"Woman, why are you weeping?"
and you heal us.
You ask, "Who touched me?"
and tell us our faith has made us well.
Touch us now as we offer our spoken and silent prayers from our hearts . . .

You do not condemn us for who we are,
for what we have done.
You love us into being,
into becoming the women we are meant to be.

We stand before you
knowing that you welcome each of us with open arms
and grace us with gifts beyond our wildest dreams.
Grant us courage to nurture one another,
wisdom to tend the seeds of our gifts.

May we share our God-given gifts with abandon
so that all may know we are indeed your beloved daughters
in whom you are well pleased.

Bless our gifts and hear our prayer
in the name of the greatest gift,
your Son, Jesus Christ. Amen.

Sue Henley

The Church Picnic Prayer

Jesus, we ask you to join us in our fun today. So many times, we come before you with need, in sorrow, or in solemn worship. Today, we want you to come and play with us. It really is that simple.

Savior, you ate and drank with those who needed you most. You blessed a wedding with happy wine and took time off from miracles to embrace children, showing us where the best miracles really are in the process. You know what it is to laugh. Please, Jesus, be in our joy, our songs, and our laughter today. Renew us with peace and innocence. Our picnic anticipates the great banquet of heaven. Glory is as near as the word of faith in our hearts. Let today be an appetizer for God's reign of love. In Jesus' name, we pray. In Jesus' name, we live. In Jesus' name, we party! Amen: let's play!

Sheryl Stewart

Prayer for Annual Meeting

God of yesterday, today, and tomorrow, we gather to plan for the year ahead and to reflect on the year past. In these twelve months we experienced a variety of chapters from the book of life. We experienced the joy and hope of birth. Our lives were enriched by the noisy enthusiasm of our youth group and the exuberance of our Sunday school.

Our church family expanded as we welcomed new members. We have been touched by the dedicated service of our staff, committees, and volunteers. Music soothed our spirits and lifted our hearts. We comforted each other in times of sorrow. We lifted up our prayers in the face of great human tragedy across the globe. We came unto you, O God, with heavy burdens and received your rest and strength.

In our church family as in every family, we encountered both grief and joy. We received your words of grace that told us that we are loved, forgiven, and cherished. Now we stand poised to welcome in a new church year. Bless us once more that we may endeavor to share your light and promise, near and far. In Jesus' name we pray. Amen.

Susan J. Foster

∾

CELEBRATION OF THE CHURCH USING CIRCUS IMAGERY

Call to Worship (several voices)

Come one, come all—step right up
to God's amazing and spectacular—church!
Come one, come all—there are seats for everyone—
    young and old, wise and foolish,
    all the colors of human skin,
    all the languages of human prayer,
    the musical and the artistic,
    dream-makers and detail-chasers,
    brisk walkers and wheelchair rollers,
    signers, speakers, and readers of Braille,
    the daring and the caring,
    the joyful, the doubting, and the sad.
Come one, come all—there are seats for everyone—
    in the shelter of God's wide tent . . .
    within the circus and the circle
    of the people of God.

Invocation · Psalm 104, loosely

Bless God, O my soul, for you have stretched out the heavens like a tent, and set
your tightrope on the waters. You make the clouds your chariots and ride on the
trapeze of the wind. You give life to the wild animals—they dance in the rings
of your creation, and roar out your majesty. You set our lives in a place of wonder and sawdust, and you cover all our deep falling with nets of safety. Amen.

Litany

We give you thanks for the three-ring church.

For the acrobatics of worship—the heights of joy, the depths of serenity,
    and all the ways we reach out to catch one another.

We give you thanks for the three-ring church.

For the juggling of committee life and calendars and agendas,
    for the way we keep the balls of music and mission,
    fellowship and stewardship, in the air at one time.

We give you thanks for the three-ring church.

For the sideshows where our hearts are touched—
    the weddings and memorials, baptisms and confirmations,

the Christmas pageant and the Rally Day festivity.

We give you thanks for the three-ring church.

For the tightropes of our many points of view
and the way we trust one another to balance,
usually with an audience.

We give you thanks for the three-ring church.

For the clowning for Christ that is church school
and youth ministry and children's sermon.

We give you thanks for the three-ring church.

For the "greatest show on earth," which is our music
that stirs courage, prays twice, eases sorrow.

We give you thanks for the three-ring church.

For the roustabouts—the staff and officers
who hammer the tent pegs of new programs,
shovel out heaps of trouble . . .
and on whom the safety of all depends.

We give you thanks for the three-ring church.

For the issues of justice where church meets world
that sometimes call for a human pyramid
and sometimes for a leap through fire.

We give you thanks for the three-ring church.

For the peanuts of detail and the elephant of budget,
for the unashamed barkers of evangelism,
the sword swallowers of reconciliation,
and the people tamers of prayer.

We give you thanks for the three-ring church.

Benediction

May you be blessed in the three rings of your life
by the Juggler of the stars,
by the Clown who is Christ,
and by the Holy Spirit—
awesome as the high wire,
intimate as a child's small hand.
Amen.

Maren C. Tirabassi

Corporate Prayer of Lament for a "Dying" Church

O God much to be worshipped,
    the Holy Spirit swept through the Upper Room and created your church,
    a community of faith charged with spreading the gospel of Jesus Christ
    to all nations.
You have asked the church to make disciples and
    transform the world through your saving power.
You have walked with the faithful to create, grow, and sustain
    the church communities.

But our church is dying.
We have been faithful.
We have studied your Word.
We have shared our resources with others.
We have testified to the good news in our lives.
We have invited our neighbors to be in community with us.
Yet our church building is almost empty.

Time has not been kind.
The town is abandoned.
The road leads people in other directions.
Our voices carry into nothingness.
Our words go out unnoticed.
Do our prayers remain unheard, as well?
Does your Spirit pass by us, moving onto more fertile fields?
Are we not worthy of life in your name?
What more can we do?

We cry out to you,
    the reason for our existence,
    with our voices united in fear and expectation.
You have harvested where there was no growth;
    you have found water in the dry river bed;
    you have given direction to the leaf carried along by the current of the wind.

Make from us a new creation:
    A community of faith conformed to your vision
    and transformed by your will.
    Let us be a home for your Spirit, and a witness for your Son,
    all for your glory, O God. Amen.

Susan E. Brown

Hymn—Behold! I am Doing a New Thing Among You
For Partnership in Ministry; tune—Kresmer ·   Isaiah 43:18–31

Behold! I am doing a new thing among you;
It springs forth to vision and brings forth my peace.
The wilderness places become an oasis;
Where hope blossoms forth my light will increase.

Forget painful past, old ways set aside.
New thinking and doing in your life I name.
Bring heart, soul, and mind; live justice and find
Renewal in Jesus! Emmanuel claim!

Where nothing has flourished a river will flow.
I feed roots that deeply you place near the source.
A blessing I'm granting, with every new planting,
Disciples who commit to stay straight the course.

My holiness seen in the everyday round,
Imagine the wonder of faith given voice!
Beloved, come forth, from sin and death restored.
My grace is all sufficient in which to rejoice.

Discerning my wisdom breaks open your fear
Of hearing from others the Christ-bearing Word,
Evangelization, from a partner congregation
Transparent in witness with honesty heard.

Behold! I am doing a new thing among you,
New ministry strengthened by joint prayer raised,
Fresh seasons unfolding, shared hopes you're beholding;
My Spirit, delights in your gathering praise.

Mark A. Rideout

Called to Ministry

A hymn written for the occasion of the Ordination of Lori Miller Lewis; tune CWM Rhondda

God, you call us to your service, call to claim our ministry.
You have given Christ as servant, helping us serve faithfully.
We respond then, each uniquely—we are all in ministry.
We are all in ministry.

You call us to share the good news, share with love so joyfully
that all people may have blessings, may live life so full and free.
That's the good news. Shout the good news! We are your evangelists.
We are your evangelists.

God you ask us to take care of all created by your hand—
care for planet, birds and flowers, all your people, every land.
We are striving to be careful, We are stewards of your gifts.
We are stewards of your gifts.

Taught by Christ, we all are teachers, reaching out to young and old.
Let us nurture truth and justice molded by the faith we hold.
We are teachers, we are learners, growing through your loving Word,
Growing through your loving Word.

Now we call upon your Spirit, Holy Spirit, come and claim
this your servant, gifted, faithful, this your child whom we ordain.
We lay hands and feel your power, power for special ministry.
Power for special ministry.

Christ calls us to serve God's people. We each have our ministry.
As we labor, as we worship, we seek global harmony.
God we praise you, God, we thank you, for your gifts of ministry.
For your gifts of ministry.

Earl D. Miller

Stewardship Serenity Prayer

God, grant me the awareness of all I have been given—the courage to give
back in full measure—and the wisdom to see both of these as blessings.

God, grant me the awareness of all I have been given—the courage to give back
in full measure—and the wisdom to be grateful for both of these blessings.

God, grant me the awareness of all I have been given—the courage to give
back in full measure—and the wisdom to gratefully acknowledge gifts given
and received as blessings.

Mary Taylor

Dedication

Creator of Every Good Gift, bless these offerings. Help us know while we can never pay you back, we can give enough to feel joy. Amen.

Priscilla L. Denham

Stewardship Prayer · Malachi 3:6–12; Mark 12:38–44

God, like little children we toddle to you, offering you a tiny gift we have bought with your money—and expecting a perfect world in return. Help us to grow up in the faith—to grow up into the faith of the widow, who gave out of her lack, knowing that letting go of all she had would challenge you to rain down blessing on her in abundance. Knowing that letting go of all she had would empty her hands to receive more. Knowing that letting go of all she had would free her mind and soul to truly love creation without owning any part of it.

God, we tithe not just our money and goods to you today, but long to tithe the more intangible things we hold on to that you demand of us.

You demand that we give up our worry and anxiety, and yet we cling to it. Help us to release the images of the six o'clock news, distorted images of violence, abuse, and abduction. Help us to release the fear we constantly live in that something terrible will happen to us or to those we love.

You demand that we give up our anger and our prejudice, so that you can defuse it and beat the swords of our minds and actions into plowshares of peaceful living, reaching out in love and acceptance to all your children: of every color, sexual orientation, age, religion—the stranger in our land and the homeless person, even to the criminal, who deserves our love and compassion.

You demand that we give up our insecurities, so that we may become people of courage and confidence who don't sell ourselves or others short. Help us to see ourselves as you have made us, so that we are challenged to do great things for the good news of Jesus Christ—ordinary people made extraordinary by our faith and conviction. Not one of us is exempt from this call. Amen.

Molly Phinney Baskette

Call to Offering · Psalm 96

"Bring an offering and come into God's courts; worship God in holy splendor," says the psalmist. How amazing! We can offer God something. This is God's generosity to us—we can share with God in the giving and receiving of gifts.

Prayer of Dedication

God, we bring these gifts—a portion of our lives,
and in this offering find ourselves not lessened,
but newly worthy, truly wealthy, and deeply blessed. Amen.

Maren C. Tirabassi

DEDICATIONS

God of Abundance, these offerings and our words are not enough to say thank you, so please accept what we give today and grow our hearts so that our offerings may blossom tomorrow. Help us discover the wild, sweet joy in giving that we find in you. Amen.

Priscilla L. Denham

Dear God, our offering exceeds what is visible here. Captured in coins and bits of paper are the hours of our days, the strength of our arms, the skill of our hands, and the talent of our imaginations. Beside, around, and within these material gifts are our silent prayers. Physical eyes do not see this reality but you see it. Please, Holy God, bless this moment of our giving that it might inform each successive instant with divine purpose. May we be a part of the mission of holy love in our community and our world. May we magnify your name. Amen.

Sheryl Stewart

Luke 21:1–4

Gracious God, Eternal Source of all good gifts,
You call us, your church, to share all that we have and all that we are with one another and the world. We remember the story of the widow who gave two small coins and know that you are more concerned with how we give than how much. Bless each offering, that together they may bring your kingdom into being in the broken places here and beyond. In Jesus' name we pray. Amen.

Sue Henley

God, receive these gifts—and give us open hands.
Fill our lives—and give us open hearts.
Touch us with prophecy—and give us open minds.
Bless this church—and give us open doors. Amen

Maren C. Tirabassi

John 6:9

God of All, we have given our money as a tangible expression of what is in
our hearts. In your hands, both money and hearts are made more alive. We
offer them as our "loaves and fish," to be multiplied and shared in a world
starving for your fierce grace. Amen.

Priscilla L. Denham

Stewardship Skit

*Scene: A small card table made to look like a kitchen table; a phone is present.
Woman sits in chair wearing a gardening outfit and facing the audience. An
empty chair represents her spouse. Feel free to use appropriate names for your
congregation.*

Boy, I'm tired this morning . . . yeah, need a cup of coffee . . . need to wake
up so I can weed the garden . . . *(as if interrupted by husband)* . . . "Yeah, I
know today's Sunday . . . not going to church . . . I'll go next Sunday . . . I said
that last Sunday? I know, but I really will go next Sunday. This garden has to
be weeded.

Monday? On Monday, duh—you know this—that's my wash day. I get the
washing done . . . then my soap is on and Dr. Phil is on at three o'clock and
I can't miss him . . . so I just better get busy . . .

Phone rings. Oh, there goes the phone. No, don't you answer it, I'll get it myself.

Hello . . . Helen? . . . We're just fine. . . . Just ready to get down on our knees
and say our morning prayers. That is we were going to take care of the garden . . . flowers, everything.

Was I in church last Sunday? . . . hmmm . . . let me see . . . yeah, um, I was in
church . . .

The sermon? . . . Oh you know . . . it's always about sin and evil and stuff like that . . . more specific? . . . Well, let's see . . . you know . . . it's usually the same thing. The pastor always says . . . you should be more Christian and all this . . . but it was good. He gives a good sermon . . . yeah, usually has a joke. We're all very busy down here . . .

How do we like our new pastor? Oh, you mean Pastor Dan . . . I like him . . . but you know what, sometimes he gets long-winded. Church is supposed to start at 10:30 and get over at 11:30, and sometimes he goes five minutes over . . . you know, the seats are kind of hard to sit on, and by 11:30 everyone's ready for a cup of coffee.

You talked to Dean last week? . . . and Dick? . . . well, I don't know if you can rely on those guys a lot, they always sit at the back of the church . . . but I do hear them say the Lord's Prayer and they both sing . . .

Yes, I sit right in front of them, but I really pay attention. I listen to everything Pastor has to say . . . yeah, it's busy, busy, busy all the time here . . .

Do I believe in gossip? . . . heavens, no. But some of the women in church do, and so do some of the men . . . Me? never.

Carol Johnson? I'm sure she misses him. but she's doing fine . . . Lonely? Oh no, she's not lonely. I can see her front door from my kitchen window and every night about a quarter to seven a gentleman comes to pick her up. Sometimes she doesn't come home until after ten . . .

Do we give money to the church? . . . Sure . . . We give money to the church . . .

Tithe? . . . Oh no, that's way too much money. Last year we gave $58, that's a little over a dollar a Sunday. I know because I took a deduction.

Yeah, we are probably too busy for a visit, but thanks for calling. You were lucky to catch me at home at this time. Yeah. Usually in church, you know. *(Hangs up phone. Lets out a sigh, as if tired by the call)*

Well, I better get to that garden if we want to go out in the new boat this afternoon.

Roena Wamberg

15

ON THE STREET
Liturgy for Civic Concerns and Occasions

WHAT SHOULD I DO THEN? I WILL PRAY
WITH THE SPIRIT, BUT I WILL PRAY WITH
THE MIND ALSO; I WILL SING PRAISE
WITH THE SPIRIT, BUT I WILL SING PRAISE
WITH THE MIND ALSO. OTHERWISE, IF YOU
SAY A BLESSING WITH THE SPIRIT, HOW CAN
ANYONE IN THE POSITION OF AN OUTSIDER
SAY THE "AMEN" TO YOUR THANKSGIVING,
SINCE THE OUTSIDER DOES NOT KNOW
WHAT YOU ARE SAYING.

1 Corinthians 14:15–16

A Litany of Labor

Ruler of the heavens, who came to earth as a humble carpenter, hear our prayers this Labor Day weekend: We give thanks for the gift of work, which can help give meaning and purpose to our lives, and which can offer us a way to serve you.

Companion of our labor, hear our prayer.

We pray for all whose work is truly their calling, that they may continue to find joy in their labor, and through their labor be drawn closer to you.

Joy in our lives, hear our prayer.

We pray for all whose work is not a joy, who work simply because they must, and who suffer boredom and exhaustion from jobs that do nothing to feed their spirits.

Source of all meaning, hear our prayer.

We pray for all whose work leads them into ethical conflicts, who struggle to do what is right in the midst of frustrating circumstances.

Guide for our path, hear our prayer.

We pray for all who are unemployed, who face daily the financial and personal anxieties that unemployment brings, who begin to wonder about their worth in the world.

Savior in the stress, hear our prayer.

We pray for all who are retired, those who enjoy retirement, those who have lost purpose in their lives, and those who struggle to make a faithful use of their days.

Teacher of quietness, hear our prayer.

We know, Gracious God, that our lives depend on the faithful labor of other workers, often those who are underpaid and overworked. Keep us aware of how our choices affect the labor of others. May all of our work be done in a way that brings you honor and glory. We pray in the name of Jesus.

Amen.

Nancy Light Gottshall

Labor Day Confession · Deuteronomy 5:6–21, Psalm 90

Surround us, O God.
Breathe into us freshness
      and self-love
           and life-joy.
We work so hard to satisfy you,
    to satisfy ourselves,
    to satisfy those around us.
We are weary of falling short and feeling incompetent.

Surround us, O God.
Breathe into us freshness
      and self-love
           and life-joy.
We want to feel useful in our community,
    intentional in our work,
    and successful in contributing to life.
Remind us that you have blessed us with gifts and skills.

Surround us, O God.
Breathe into us freshness
    and self-love
        and life-joy.

Rachel G. Hackenberg

Blessing for a Small Town Parade on Labor Day Weekend

To the One we call by many names, on this day you call us to be in community and to be in celebration in this town center that is loved by many. We ask for your blessing upon all those gathered here: those who call this town home and those visiting today, parade movers-and-shakers and onlookers, even the four-legged creatures and the moving vehicles and farm machinery. May all gathered be enveloped in the spirit of play and excitement, doing and being, work and leisure on this holiday weekend. In gratitude, journey forward! Go in peace!

Elizabeth D. Barnum

Election Week Invocation · Psalm 72

Give our elected officials your justice, O God.

And your righteousness to all who follow them in office.

May they judge your people with righteousness, and give justice to your poor.

**May these mountains yield prosperity for all who reside here,
and our rivers run with abundant and pure water.**

May our leaders speak up for those whose voices have been silenced.

And may they gather to the table of abundance all who have been excluded.

Kenneth L. Sehested

Civic New Year Prayer

Holy and Loving God, we thank you for the beautiful [desert] setting of our city and for the water that we *do* have. Thank you for human government that makes our society possible. Thank you for the administration and services of justice, safety, education, recreation, health, and well-being that come to us through our city government. Thank you for the privilege and ability of our citizens and businesses to pay taxes and so to have a share and say in this governance. Thank you for these your particular children and gifted servants, whom we, the people, have elected to govern us. We ask you to guide them by your spirit within them, as their vision, planning, and decision-making affect not only them and their families, but all of us together—and even our future as a city. So it is that we ask for today's agenda and deliberations—and in all their meeting and thoughts—that you would give this mayor and this council and all those who serve the city of [Phoenix] the degree of humility, wisdom, and courage they will need to help us to be and become all that we are meant to be.

You are the source of all the hope that is: we ask you to spare these your servants from both the cynicism and burnout that ever-threaten those in public service. Save them from those temptations of pride and self-aggrandizement that plague us all and cause us to be and do less than our best.

In this New Year of your grace, bless these, our elected officials and their support staffs, with a love for this city and for all that it is and all that it may yet become. Bless them with vision and dreams and hopes for [Phoenix] that are both realistic and extravagant. Bless them with amazement at this city's wondrous diversity. Bless them, above all else, with love and compassion for all this city's people, young and old, rich and poor, black, brown, and white, gay and straight, those with disabilities and those temporarily able-bodied, the sick and the well, the native and the immigrant, the documented and the desperate—bless the members of this council with love and compassion for all people of whatever political party or stripe, and of whatever religion or denomination, for we are all your children. For some larger purpose, in your wisdom and grace, you have placed us all together in this one city at this time and place. May we be a blessing to one another. As a Christian I pray in *that* name, yet in this room we know you in many ways. So we ask this blessing by whatever way or name we call you, in great confidence that you hear and love us all. Amen.

Stephen E. Wayles

Prayer in Many Voices for Mother's Day

To be prayed by representatives of the diversity of gender, age, race, and family configurations of the congregation speaking from different places.

VOICE ONE: Loving God, the prophets have spoken of how you are a mother to us: giving us life, teaching us the way to go, correcting us when wrong, feeding and nurturing us with good things. We are grateful for all your mothering, not only of us, but of all your creation.

VOICE TWO: We thank you for our own mothers, those who gave us life, those who raised and taught us, those who sacrificed for us. Help us to forgive the times our mothers failed us or hurt us. If our mothers have died, we pray they rest from their labors in the peace of your love.

VOICE THREE: We ask your blessings and help for all who are mothers. Give them partners along the way, for no one can raise a child alone. Bring healing and help to those mothers who have lost their way and abuse their children. Bring peace to those mothers who have had to relinquish their children to be raised by family or adoptive parents.

VOICE FOUR: Bless those who give so much as foster mothers, and grant them the support and resources they need to keep the children in their care healthy and strong. Give help and hope to those women seeking to be mothers who suffer from infertility; especially on this day they need your warm embrace in their pain. And be with those awaiting children by adoption that they might be graced with patience and trust. Bless those who are pregnant and awaiting motherhood that their pregnancies might be healthy and their spirits patient as well.

VOICE FIVE: Be especially with women the world over who are struggling to raise children in the midst of war, of poverty, of oppression, of fear. Be with refugees, the homeless, those caught in abusive relationships.

VOICE SIX: Strengthen mothers of all nations whose children are soldiers or work in other dangerous professions as they fear for their safety daily. Comfort all mothers whose children have died or are seriously ill, and help them to lean on you.

VOICE SEVEN: Help us as members of this church to take our baptismal promises seriously and act as godmothers and godfathers to the children of this church and as supports to their parents. May we remember always that we are all children of one God.

VOICE EIGHT: Grant that all mothers everywhere may hold dear those moments of sheer joy in the presence of their children, never taking them for granted, but thanking you for the privilege of raising your children. Bless all mothers that they might be parents in your image; help them to reach out to you, remembering that you know what it is like to mother the world.

ALL: In Jesus' name we pray, Amen.

Rochelle A. Stackhouse

Prayer For Father's Day

To be prayed by representatives of the diversity of gender, age, race, and family configurations of the congregation speaking from different places.

VOICE ONE: Loving God, whom Jesus called Abba, Daddy, we come to you as your children this day, with love, with sorrow for the times we have not loved as we should, with many requests for your loving, fathering presence in our lives and in our world. Thank you for being there, for listening, for holding us with gentle power when we are weak, for pushing us to be the best we can be.

VOICE TWO: Thank you for our earthly fathers today. Thank you for their care, their support, their nurture, and their love. Help us to forgive the mistakes they have made and let the past be past. Help them, likewise, to forgive the mistakes we have made that have hurt them. For we know that being a father is challenging work.

VOICE THREE: Bless all fathers today. Strengthen those who deal with difficult or handicapped children, those who are single fathers trying to be both mother and father to their children, those whose children are estranged from them.

VOICE FOUR: Bless those who desperately want to be fathers and are having difficulty, those whose partners are pregnant, those in the adoption process. Give wisdom to those who are foster fathers, godfathers, grandfathers, uncles, and others who are acting as father to children. Bless all the men of this congregation as they fulfill their baptismal promises to be godfathers to all the children of this church.

VOICE FIVE: Soften the hearts of fathers who abuse, either children or the children's mothers. Give courage to fathers who find themselves in the midst of war, as soldiers, as beleaguered civilians, as refugees. Be with those fathers who are unemployed or underemployed and lack the resources they need to support their families. Be especially with those whose desperation tempts them to desert their families, that they might think again and stay.

VOICE SIX: Bless all married couples, those with or without children, that they might be strengthened in love and commitment to one another. And help our society, both government and private enterprise, to do what needs to be done to support families of whatever configuration to nurture and care for one another.

VOICE SEVEN: Hear us now as we pray for our own fathers, marriages, and families in the silence of the morning.

Voice Seven: In Jesus' name, let all the people say,

All: Amen and amen.

Rochelle A. Stackhouse

Independence Day Prayer

God of Peace and Justice, we rest in your presence on this day of celebration and remembrance, mindful of the work of our forebears in securing for us certain inalienable civil rights endowed by you at the creation. We know that we have not always lived up to those glorious standards that we have set for ourselves and that you call us to, that we have not always put first the cause of justice but instead our own petty grievance. We have pursued our own pleasure at the cost of the life, liberty, or pursuit of happiness of our brother or sister.

We pray for your presence in the institutions of our civilization, in our nation's leaders and lawmakers, in our local government, in our school systems and in our businesses. May you invest in all of these human institutions a sense of divine justice, the freedom that invites us to be responsible for every human being's dignity and well-being. We pray for your vigilant presence in the governments on every continent of the world that still oppress their peoples based on religious expression, or race, or gender. We pray that we might know what you know: that until all are free, none is free.

We pray for your presence in our families and communities, that the ties that bind us not be burdensome but freely chosen bonds of interdependence upon one another. We pray we might become more grateful for each other, as gifts from you, each made in your image but made wonderfully different from each other.

We pray for your presence in those who are sick or those who have lost someone recently to death. May your hand of healing rest upon them and free them from illness, if not from illness then from pain, if not from pain then from fear, that they may dwell secure in the knowledge that as certainly as suffering is a part of them, so are you an even deeper part of them.

We pray for your presence in our own lives. Help us to declare independence from those thoughts and behaviors and allegiances that keep us from being wholly yours. Invite us to be free of blame, anxiety, guilt, rage, and fear toward ourselves and others. Leave room in our hearts for nothing but love, so that we might experience ourselves as already liberated.

Molly Phinney Baskette

Independence Day Confession

The roots of our freedom were planted in this soil by our Pilgrim forbearers who believed that Jesus means freedom. That conviction did not always save them from fear and prejudice, nor does is always save us. But it can be where we start and start again. Jesus demands of us the courage to love those whom we naturally fear. Let us pray.

O God, we have not always been equal to the task. We have relied on superior force and dire threats, when love alone has the power to turn an enemy into a friend and secure our safety. Forgive us, we pray in Jesus name. Amen.

Assurance

Do not fear—the lust of nations shall be overcome by the love of God, and you shall be love's courier. The narrowness of your love shall be broken open by the breadth of God's kindness toward you. Nor will God allow the sins of your past to keep you from the task God has for you, for in all things the ultimate victory belongs to Christ, and he has overcome the world.

David Slater

16

AT THE CROSSROADS
Liturgy for Justice Issues and
Open and Affirming Resources

"CURSED BE ANYONE WHO DEPRIVES
THE ALIEN, THE ORPHAN, AND
THE WIDOW OF JUSTICE."
ALL THE PEOPLE SHALL SAY, "AMEN!"

Deuteronomy 27:19

Invitation to Offering

God is present in the mountains and deserts, the cities and countryside, in places of horror and places of peace. God laughs with us, mourns with us, and calls us to work for justice. God calls us to change and grow. God's love is with us every day of our lives. Let us share our gifts with God through the morning offering.

Frances A. Bogle

Call to Worship

In caring and compassion, God's arms hold us when we are weak

With ideas and inspiration, God pushes us to grow and thrive.

With divine generosity, God shares all creation with us.

God calls us as partners to build a world of joy and hope.

Let us join our hearts, hands, and voices with people the world over in praise, thanksgiving, and commitment to our one, our wondrous God.

Benediction · Isaiah 61

The Spirit of God is upon us!

**By the power of God ruined cities and devastated lands
shall be repaired and rebuilt.**

By the power of God the broken shall be healed, the oppressed freed,
and those who mourn, comforted.

By the power of God we are anointed as partners in this work of love.

The Spirit of God is upon us;
go forth to work and praise, made new by the power of God.

Rochelle A. Stackhouse

In the midst of turbulent lives and turbulent times, we gather in the name of Jesus, your risen one, to proclaim the wonder of your stone-moving love. With praise in our hearts and thanksgiving on our tongues, Holy One, we celebrate your life-giving, life-changing energy. Call us forth from self-defined tombs and lead us into resurrection. Open our hearts to the brilliance of life undefined by personal failure and regret. Then in your mercy awaken us to the responsibilities new life demands. Lead us from death to life, from fear to faith, from war to peace, for even in our most difficult hours we seek the better angels of our nature. Proclaiming Jesus as perfector of our faith, we seek to live as he lived: full of grace, telling truth, and risking all for the sake of your realm. for the sake of justice this day, for the sake of grace this day, may it be so. Amen.

June Goudey

Prayer of Confession

Merciful God,
we have not obeyed your holy laws.

We have not respected your creation:
we have polluted the earth
and wasted the resources you have given us.

We have not loved our neighbors as ourselves:
we have ignored the sick, the poor, and the homeless
and abandoned the hungry.

We have not been peacemakers:
we have used our privileges for our own good
and ignored our enemies.

Forgive us, O God, and restore in us
pure hearts and minds
so that our actions
reflect your will, not ours.

All praise and glory to you, O Holy One.
Amen.

Patricia Catellier

Assurance of Grace

God, in gracious love, gives us the awareness of how far we fall short of caring for this earth and our brothers and sisters and the strength to change our lives. Forgiveness is the pivot that turns repentance into reconciliation.

Maren C Tirabassi

Invocation for a Service on Immigration Issues

Gracious One, who jealously guards the lives of those at every edge, we lift our heavy hearts to your mercy.

We live in a fretful land, anxious over the ebbing away of privilege, fearful that strangers are stealing our birthright.

Loud, insistent voices demand a return to "the rule of law."

**Speak to us of the rule of your law, the terms of your reign.
Incline our hearts to your command.**

"Cursed be anyone who deprives the alien, the orphan, and the widow of justice." All the people shall say, "Amen!" (Deut. 27:19)

All the people shall say, "Amen!"

"You shall also love the stranger, for you were strangers in the land of Egypt" (Deut. 10:19).

All the people shall say, "Amen!"

"There shall be one law for the native and for the alien who resides among you" (Exod. 12:49).

All the people shall say, "Amen!"

"When an alien resides with you in your land, you shall not oppress the alien" (Lev. 19:33).

All the people shall say, "Amen!"

Then I will draw near to you for judgment; I will be swift to bear witness against . . . those who thrust aside the alien, and do not fear me, says the [God] of hosts (Mal. 3:5).

All the people shall say, "Amen!"

Speaking to those welcomed to paradise, Jesus said " I was a stranger and you welcomed me" (Matt. 25:35).

All the people shall say, "Amen!"

For we, who were formerly illegal aliens and undocumented workers in creation's midst, "are no longer strangers and aliens, but with the saints and also members of the household of God" (Eph. 2:19).

Kenneth L. Sehested

Litany Against Torture

O God, around the world voices cry out.

As bodies are broken.

O God, in dungeons, prison cells, secret sites, and pristine medical centers voices cry out.

As pain too awful to imagine is inflicted on bodies and minds.

O God, women and men are sexually abused, electrically shocked, chemically altered, terrorized by dogs, starved, beaten, and drowned.

As bodies, minds and souls are tortured in our names, we cry out: Stop the torture now.

Close the Guantanamo Bay prison camp. Close the secret CIA houses. End capital punishment. Stop sending prisoners of war to other countries so that they can be tortured at our request by someone else's hands.

Stop the torture now. It is wrong. It is evil. It is against God's will.

We believe in a God of love, hope, and justice who knows torture and death on a cross, and offers life and grace to all.

In God's name, stop the torture now. Amen.

Frances A. Bogle

Confession

O God, sometimes bad things happen to good people and we don't like it. And sometimes good things happen to bad people, and we don't like that either. The corrupt don't pay for their corruption, widows and orphans do, stockholders and taxpayers do. Virtue has few visible rewards, and we are tempted to conclude that dishonesty pays better. Dear God, save us, lest we buy the lie. Save us before we endanger our hearts and imperil our souls. We pray in the name of Jesus Christ. Amen.

Assurance · Galatians 6:7

"Do not be deceived, God is not mocked. For whatever a person sows that will a person reap." But know too that saints and sinners alike who, with sincere and contrite hearts call on God, shall know the mercy of God.

David Slater

A Question of Justice

My sense of justice
is profoundly shaped
by bloody water:

Great-great-grandfather,
brained and detesticled
by Lakota war hatchets,
was summarily tossed
into Currier Pond.

"His land" had historically
been treatied to natives.
He moved on it with the blessing
of "wasichu"—white man's law.

Broken treaties equaled broken bodies—
death by desperation.

In retaliation, thirty-four Lakota
were hanged—
none of whom were weapons wielders.

I often fished in what became known as Bloody Lake,
while concerted by blackbirds and meadow larks.
Local lore has it that the fish are fatter
as a result of ancestral blood.

When I consider multiple bodies
dangling
between prairie grass and horse-maned sky,
dirged by blackbirds and meadow larks

I cut my old familial ties
and strike out anew on a quest for justice.

Roger Robbennolt

We Give Thanks for An Ordinary Day

We give thanks for water, refreshing, cleansing,
And pray for those who have no running water.

We give thanks for electricity, to make our morning tea and coffee,
for the refrigerator, the hairdryer,
And pray for the coffee farmers, for fair trade, for those with no electricity.

As we drop trash into the bin and go to the dumpster,
We pray for those who seek food in dumpsters, or hide in them to keep warm.

As we give our pets water and food, we delight in their presence
And pray for animals who are neglected, whose habitat is being destroyed.

As we inhale the beauty of the morning mountains and trees,
We pray for the places of deforestation and give thanks for Wangari
Maathai, tree-planter, Nobel Peace Prize winner.

As we get in our cars, we give thanks for transportation,
And pray for those who walk, for injustices in our world created around oil.
As we drive to work, we give thanks that we have work,
And pray for the unemployed.

We take the call from the doctor's office, telling us the test was just fine,
And pray for those whose results are not just fine, and those who have no
access to medical care, or no health insurance.

We give thanks for friends who visit, sharing a simple meal,
And pray for the friendless and those who always eat alone.

As we go to bed, we give thanks for rest, for a place called home,
And we pray for those who live in shelters, whose homes are destroyed
by war and violence.
And we give thanks for another Ordinary Day.

Sue Henley

A World That Is Good

We celebrate the goodness of life and the world
All persons' goodness and their diversity
All relationships that promote love
All love that is caring and outreaching
All justice for human rights
All churches who are Open and Affirming
All gay, lesbian, bisexual and transgender persons
All the human family together without fear
All borders without walls or death
All nations that lay down their weapons
All extended family values without fundamentalist morals
All stem cell research to give new life
All public education with human freedom
All environmental care to conserve the earth
All justice without the death penalty
All gun control without limit
All individual choices for women
All health care for everyone
All children loved and not abused
We must be a Presence of Justice to all of God's children

Fletcher D. Wideman

PRAYERS FOR AN OPEN AND AFFIRMING (ONA) PROCESS

Beginning · Hebrews 11:1–12

Gracious God, guide of your people through the generations, like Sarah and Abraham, we set off in response to your Spirit, not knowing exactly where we are going.

Some of us can hardly wait to begin; some of us wonder if we should.

Many are our hopes, our concerns, our questions about discussing sexuality and gender, inclusion and justice, and what this all means for our church's life and witness. Accompany us, we pray, as we speak and listen, learn and unlearn together.

Open our hearts, help us always to care for one another and honor your image in each person. By faith, we go forward. Center us, deepen us, and lead us on each step of this journey, that who we are and what we do may embody the love of Christ. Amen.

Deciding · Ephesians 4:15–16

Spirit of God, we give you thanks for the days of preparation that have brought us to this moment. Seeking always to do your good will, we lift up in prayer our decision about making an Open and Affirming witness.

We have been challenged and blessed by learning and reflecting together.

We thank you for all who gave of themselves as leaders and participants in this process, for all who raised questions and all who shared stories of their lives. We have tried to speak the truth in love and help one another grow up in Christ. If, along this way, we have caused hurt, help us forgive and heal. Nurture, we pray, the unfolding wisdom of our hearts and minds.

Grant that through the action we take together now, we may become more truly the body of Christ in this time and place.

We wait upon you. Speak to our hearts.

Silence

In this and all things, loving God,
may we be your faithful people,
honoring your name and blessing your world. Amen.

Witnessing · Romans 15:1–13

We are an Open and Affirming community of faith!

Varied in gender and sexual orientation,
    color and age, ethnicity and ability,
    we are a widening circle,
    open to all who seek Christ,
    a rainbow company,
    affirming the splendor of our humanity.

Melding strengths and weaknesses,
    we serve one another and the world
    as Christ serves us.

Encouraged by scripture and fashioned by Spirit,
    we endeavor to live in harmony
    and to do justice,
    in accordance with Christ Jesus.

As an Open and Affirming body of Christ, we intend:

to welcome one another,
    just as Christ has welcomed us,
    equally and jubilantly,
    for the glory of God!

As an Open and Affirming body of Christ, we pray:

God of hope, by the power of your Holy Spirit,
    fill us with joy and peace in believing,
    that we may abound in hope
    and live the vision we proclaim!

Amen.

Ann B. Day

A Prayer for Transgender Brothers and Sisters

Appropriate for the Annual Transgender Day of Remembrance—annually held on November 20

When, O Gentle God, do our differently gendered brothers and sisters find peace and security in their lives?

When, O Loving Spirit, can we stop holding annual memorial services across the world to "Remember our Dead," killed simply because they were transgender?

When, O Compassionate Christ, will transgender persons be welcomed and judged on the basis of what they do with their lives rather than on how they present themselves to the world?

We find it easy to pray with faith-filled confidence to the Trinity, three persons in one God. Yet we ignore, ridicule, or even persecute those who embody a dichotomy of gender in their lives.

Help us to overcome our unbelief and skepticism and to understand the beautiful workings of our triune God in the lives of our transgender sisters and brothers.

Barbara Satin

OPEN AND AFFIRMING RESOURCES

Call to Worship

We come together in a rainbow of hope and love.

We come together with fear and trembling for the new world we are creating.

With open arms, with pride and joy, we welcome people from every nation and ethnic community into our church. Gay, lesbian, bisexual, transgender, queer, questioning, same-gender-loving, straight, old, young, disabled, athletes, people with questions, and those who know the answers—all are welcome here.

No one is excluded from Christ's table.

God loves us all.

We are one in the Spirit! Alleluia! Amen.

Confession

Gracious, loving God, we open our hearts to you. We confess that there have been times when we have turned away from you. There have been times when we have hurt and rejected our neighbors. Sometimes it has been difficult to love and accept ourselves. All of us have participated in the systemic oppressions that are part of our culture. Forgive us for our racism, sexism, homophobia, and economic elitism. Give us the courage to stand up for the dignity and rights of all of our sisters and brothers. Make us willing to change our lives in response to your call to love our neighbors and to create a world of peace and justice for all of your beloved. In Jesus name we pray, Amen.

Words of Assurance

Friends, God hears our confessions with an ever merciful and loving heart and forgives us over and over again. Nothing can separate us from the love of God. Let us rejoice in this good news. Amen.

Invitation to offering

Friends, on this day of pride and joy let us share our gifts or time, talent, and money with our church and the world.

Dedication

Spirit of openness and affirmation, we dedicate these gifts to the ministry of love and acceptance in the world. May we ever seek to use all of our resources to create a world and a church where all are welcome and honored, loved and fully known. This we pray in the name of Jesus, who welcomed everyone to his table. Amen.

Invitation to Offering

Let us share of gifts with pride and joy as we remember that God loves each one of us and Jesus welcomes us around this table. There are no strangers here. We are all one in the Spirit of love.

Dedication

God of hope and welcome, we dedicate these gifts of time, money, and prayer to you. Bless us as we share our lives and stories as lesbians, gay men, transgender, bisexual, queer, questioning, same-gender-loving, and heterosexual people with the world. Help us use all of our gifts to make this planet a place of safety and welcome for all of your beloved. In Jesus name we pray. Amen.

Benediction

May the God whose loves fill us with peace and joy bless us as we go forth to do the work of justice in the world. Our service has ended, our service begun. Amen.

Benediction (alternate)

May the God of the rainbow bless and fill us with hope, strength, joy, and peace as we go forth to do the work of love in the world. Never forget that as we open our hearts and affirm our love, God is with us, now and forever, and Jesus walks beside us on our journey. Walk gently and in peace, friends in Christ. Amen.

Frances A. Bogle

God's Rainbow People · Genesis 9:12–13, Micah 6:8

May be used for weddings/unions

VOICE ONE: For our storm-tossed world, the rainbow is a sign of hope.

VOICE TWO: For communities that embrace and affirm the spectrum of sexual orientation and gender identity, the rainbow is a sign of welcome, pride, and justice.

VOICE ONE: For many persons of faith, the rainbow is also a powerful sign of the enduring relationship between the Holy and humankind. We remember that, according to the book of Genesis, God said to Noah . . .

VOICE TWO: "This is the sign of the covenant that I make between me and you and every living creature that is with you for all future generations. I have set my bow in the clouds, and it shall be a sign of the covenant between me and the earth."

ALL: **In God's sight all humankind is a rainbow people! Many and splendid are we—in color and culture, sexuality and gender, ability and language—shining together beneath the arching colors of Divine love!**

VOICE ONE: *Red*—color of strawberry and rose petal, passion and birth.

Voice Two: Sweet and vivacious, color of life: Red.

VOICE ONE: God of life, we thank you for the breaths we take, for urban energies and rural rhythms, for day's demands and night's repose, and for your care surrounding all.

VOICE TWO: Especially, this day, we thank you for the blessings and challenges of right-relationship, for love configured in myriad ways—with friends and families, sweethearts and partners, coworkers, neighbors, and even enemies.

ALL: **Guide us through love's complexities. Empower us to shape a world where love may flourish—a world without poverty, violence, and discrimi-**

nation—a world in which all children are cherished, all elders are esteemed, all couples are free to marry, and vows exchanged anywhere are respected everywhere.

VOICE TWO: *Orange*—color of pumpkin and flame, warmth and compassion.

VOICE ONE: Bright and enlivening, color of healing: Orange.

VOICE TWO: God of healing, we trust you are at work in our bodies and families, neighborhoods and nations to bring health and restoration.

ALL: Uphold all who live with hunger, loneliness, illness, and grief; all who live in the midst of danger or in exile; all who wonder how they will manage another day. Uphold us as we offer comfort and advocate for change. Uproot our indifference and plant in us the strength to be aware, compassionate, and just.

VOICE ONE: *Yellow*—color of lemon and sun, joy and enthusiasm.

VOICE TWO: Radiant and bold, color of hope: Yellow.

VOICE ONE: God of hope, we bless you for creation's unfolding, for mysteries around us and potential within us, for goodness called forth as we live with faith, forgiveness, and generosity.

ALL: Nurture these graces in us, that we may be channels of your transforming power.

VOICE TWO: *Green*—color of inchworm and pine, calm and growth.

VOICE ONE: Restful and abundant, color of nature: Green.

VOICE TWO: God of the universe, we rejoice in the splendors and sustenance of our planet—its woods and waters, deserts and fields, peaks and valleys—and in all, seen and unseen, that lives upon it.

ALL: Give us wisdom to act with care and respect for this our earthly home.

VOICE ONE: *Blue*—color of sky and mountain ridge, depth and inspiration.

VOICE TWO: Soaring and fluent—color of harmony: Blue.

VOICE ONE: God of harmony, we know that you intend our differences to enrich and not divide us.

ALL: Help us to listen and to learn from one another. Move us to bring down barriers of prejudice and raise up bridges of understanding. Set our hearts upon shalom and give us courage in the struggles for justice and peace.

VOICE TWO: *Purple*—color of grape and lilac, strength and dignity.

VOICE ONE: Profound and majestic—color of spirit: Purple.

VOICE TWO: God, eternal Spirit, we praise you! Thanks be to you for all who have come before us, blazing paths of equality and community.

VOICE ONE: Thanks be to you for those today who, in word and action, respond to your call to love kindness, do justice, and live humbly with you.

ALL: God, eternal Spirit, we praise you! With your rainbow spread over us, send us forth to be your Spirited people! May your love shine through us, now and always, Amen!

Five of the color connotations in the litany—life, healing, nature, harmony, and spirit—are among those noted by Gilbert Baker, who designed the first eight-striped Rainbow Flag in 1978. They have been expanded upon and adapted for this litany. The rainbow is the most recognized symbol of communities that include and affirm persons who identify as lesbian, bisexual, gay, same-gender-loving, transgender, two-spirit, intersex, queer, and questioning, by other names or none at all.

Ann B. Day

17

OF HEALING AND HOPE

Liturgy Around Health and Education Concerns

MAY THE GRACE OF OUR LORD
JESUS CHRIST BE WITH YOUR SPIRIT,
BROTHERS AND SISTERS.
AMEN.

Galatians 6:18

Prayer For Healing · Psalm 18; Matthew 5:13–16

Dancing Light,
shed light on the corners of our souls
    where aches linger
        and anger builds like mold
    where memories ferment
        and self-pity licks its wounds.

Dancing Light,
brighten the shadows deep within
    where lies are hidden
        and criticism awaits its prey
    where contempt lurks
        and distrust rustles underfoot

Dancing Light,
shine upon the windows of our hearts,
>   where love should live
>>   and forgiveness be always ready
>   where hope is bright
>>   and praise ever lifts our tongues.

Rachel G. Hackenberg

Call To Worship

Are you suffering?

Some of us are tired and sick.

Are you sad?

Some of us often weep.

Are you wounded?

Some of us bear many scars.

Brothers and sisters, trust in Jesus Christ, the Great Redeemer.

As children of a loving Creator,
we can share each other's sorrows.
Let us pray for one another.
Let us praise the Holy One. Amen.

Patricia Catellier

Prayer for Undiagnosed Sickness

God of all knowledge and discovery, guide the professionals who seek to name the enemy that threatens the health of *(name of sick person)*. As we seek to assist the natural miracles of healing you have placed within [her or his] body, direct us to appropriate interventions, both traditional and alternative. Finally, beyond any care medicine and nursing may offer, touch *(name)* with the hand of [her or his] creator. May Jesus, our Great Physician, restore your child to the full health and abundant life that is your design and intent for [her or his]. We rest secure, held in the knowledge of your love. Amen.

Sheryl Stewart

Responsive Reading   ·   Genesis 1, 12, 21; Psalm 8, 139

For Access Sunday/Disabilities Awareness Week or when one of the scriptures is a lectionary reading.

ALL: God created us, reflecting God's nature.
Our Creator blessed us; God saw that all God made,
Indeed, was very good.

LEADER: Hearing well is not always an option.

PEOPLE: Trimming a mustache, facing a person directly
Or speaking with clarity is.

ALL: I will bless you so that you will be a blessing.

LEADER: To live without pain is not always an option.

PEOPLE: Offering a straight-backed padded armchair is.

ALL: I will bless you so that you will be a blessing.

LEADER: While the capacity to sit or stand for a long time is not always possible,

PEOPLE: To plan breaks or alternate activity with rest is.

ALL: We praise you,
For we are fearfully and wonderfully made.
Wonderful are your works; that we know well.

LEADER: Having full mobility is not always an option,

PEOPLE: Replacing a heavy door or offering wheelchair space within the community circle is.

ALL: We praise you,
For we are fearfully and wonderfully made.
Wonderful are your works; that we know well.

LEADER: Seeing may not always be an option,

PEOPLE: Identifying ourselves by name or describing a new space is.

ALL: We praise you,
For we are fearfully and wonderfully made.
Wonderful are your works; that we know well.

LEADER: When speaking with clarity is not an option,

PEOPLE: To ask again until I understand or to rephrase
With a yes/no question is.

ALL: God is with us in all that we do.
God saw that all God made
Indeed, was very good.

LEADER: To think clearly is not always an option

PEOPLE: To repeat or simplify is.

ALL: What are human beings that you are mindful of us,
Mortals that you care for us?
Yet you have crowned us with glory and honor.

LEADER: Relating well with others is not easy for everyone,

PEOPLE: Encouraging someone to join an activity or taking time to chat is.

ALL: What are human beings that you are mindful of us,
Mortals that you care for us?
Yet you have crowned us with glory and honor.
Blessed be God who delights in everyone. Amen.

Dallas A. (Dee) Brauninger

Learning Disorders

God of all knowledge, our society places so much value on what we know that we are misers of learning, stockpiling facts like treasured gold. *(Name)* needs help to learn. We pray that you would heal and help [him or her] uncover the excitement of knowledge, the joy of reading, and the confidence of skills that currently frustrate [her or him]. However, remind us that it is not information that you prize, O God; heaven loves wisdom and those ranked last may well teach those who think they are head of the class.

Wise souls live simple, godly lives. If we accumulated every skill and memorize all the facts, we are still poor and ignorant if we do not know our God and cannot love like Jesus. Creator, you so often choose the ones who are most empty of worldly knowledge to be filled with treasures of heavenly wisdom. Help *(name)* to learn, value, and apply the lessons of Christ. And, as *(name)* learns of heaven's hope, help [her or him] to teach us. Amen.

Sheryl Stewart

God of my life, source of my strength, and guide of my heart,
I know you are present within me.
I accept the loving grace you offer me moment by moment.
I welcome the new life that is unfolding before me,
I trust that all the wisdom I need is now present to my deep and true self.
I offer this prayer knowing that healing is at hand. And so it is. Amen.

June Goudey

Parish Nurses' Prayers

One: Creator of body, mind, and spirit, we know good health involves physical, emotional, mental, relational, spiritual, and environmental factors. We wouldn't even be here if you had not knelt in Eden and plunged creative fingers into the ground to form us. Keep us real, God. May our worship be ever grounded in practical application, our prayers working in concert with the knowledge and skills we acquire. If we start by getting folks to say "Ah," let's end up with "Amen." Make us true, O God, make us true.

Two: Thank you, Jesus, for not staying abstracted from the world in the lofty palaces of heaven. You walk among us, healing and loving. Thank you for your example of referring many of those you touched to the doctors and priests to confirm and continue God's healing process. That reminds us to collaborate.

Likewise, thank you for the times when your healing prayer was given in conjunction with an astringent application of mud and/or saliva, a common folk medicine practice of the time. This reminds us to use all the tools you give us, both spiritual and mundane miracles.

Remind us to keep the holy in holistic and ensure that the feet of our faith touch the ground. May faith and knowledge be sisters, may science and prayer be brothers, and may we all sing in the harmony of the same choir; Amen!

Sheryl Stewart

Voices of Prayer: Take Back the Night
Psalm 143:7–8; Revelation 7:13–17)

Voice One: O God, I have a secret:
It is not my secret, but it has been given to me for keeping.
It is not my secret, but she couldn't keep it, couldn't face it.
O God, I don't want this secret either.

VOICE TWO: O God, I have a secret:
She was speeding; he was protecting the law.
She was speeding, but the officer broke the law and left her unprotected.
O God, take her secret.

VOICE THREE: O God, I have a secret:
She was dancing; he was enjoying the music.
She was dancing, but her date changed his tune and enjoyed her protesting body.
O God, I wish I didn't know.

VOICE FOUR: O God, I have a secret:
She was sleeping; he was a trusted friend visiting her parents.
She was sleeping, but the uncle broke the trust and visited her in the dark.
O God, make it go away.

UNISON VOICES: O God, these are our secrets.
How long will we suffer in private humiliation?
How long will we bear this burden on our bodies?
How long will we live in a world where abusers reign?
O God, we surrender our secrets. Heal our souls. Amen.

Rachel G. Hackenberg

Breathe On Us · Ezekiel 37; Acts 2 (also appropriate for Pentecost)

The troubling breath of the Blessed One led us to this canyon of bleached bones.

Can these bones live? Can these bones live?

That Breath broke into speech: O human one, hear my question and answer rightly.

Only you know. Only you know.

Then prophesy to these skeletal remains.

O dry bones, hear the Word of the One whose breath brings refreshment.

Flesh shall follow sinew; moist skin will be stretched in supple layers.

Breathe, O dry bones, breathe again!

The rumble of life shall overwhelm the rattle of death. Graveyards shall open and spill their captives into fertile fields.

Breathe, O dry bones, breathe again! Fill your lungs with Spirit's Wind.

Sons and daughters, old ones and young, meadow and mountain, beast and bird, the One present at creation shall be honored again. On that day, no longer shall any govern by threat of the grave.

Spirit descend! Breathe on us, Breath of God.

Kenneth L. Sehested

A Prayer for Christian Educators

Jesus our teacher, Almighty God our creator, Holy Spirit our inspiration: hear our prayer. We need your help. We are meeting today to study and plan for the knee-shaking responsibility of sharing our God with our children. We love them and, impossibly, we want to give them better than our best.

Jesus, you promised that all things are possible with God. Shine though our lives, in and out of class, so that we may do more than teach facts. Help us to introduce you. Open our ears; we may learn from those we would teach. Let our discipline be fair, firm, and kind. Please, shape our classrooms into Eden's garden, where you walk among us. Only with your help may we hope for these things, Eternal Teacher. Live and breathe through all our lesson plans. Amen.

Sheryl Stewart

God of fresh dawns and new beginnings, you are at the core of all things. You wash us clean, wipe out our mistakes, and heal our wounds. Thank you for this new semester. Awaken our hearts and minds that we may learn and grow in and through your luminous creation. Let us lay down our burdens and rejoice. Amen.

Susan Hodge-Parker

Prayer before Leaving for College

Our lives are full of change and new opportunities, O God.

We pause now to give thanks for these students who are about to begin their incredible new journey at college. Teach them how to take advantage of all the opportunities that lie before them as part of the college community and the global community.

We give thanks for the families of these students whose love, support, and commitment helped them seek education. Comfort them and guide them as they continue to offer their support, perhaps even over long distances.

We give thanks for faculty and staff, whose efforts bring students to college. They work to provide a safe place to learn and grow. Accompany every single person as each journeys on his or her vocation. Thank you for new opportunities, O God. Amen.

Katherine Low

Prayer with Senior Students

Why, O God, do we think ourselves helpless when we have you to call upon? Our prayers are floodgates that may direct rivers of blessing and divine power into our world. We have spent our lives establishing the work of our hands as a heritage for our children. Yet, more than any inheritance we have forged, the blessing of the prayers we have yet to offer hold the most power to bless our children. Grant that our study and worship this day might empower our petitions, which pour out from this place to empower our children, our community, and our world.

We know our request for power in prayer shall be answered, for it is asked in full accord with the spirit of the One who has prayed for us all our lives, even Jesus Christ. Amen.

Sheryl Stewart

Confession · Luke 10:38–42

Teacher God, we offer to you the confession of Martha, the confession of busyness. Too often we have substituted serving for learning, acting for being. We have forgotten to befriend the silence of our souls, to soak in the power of your love, to receive the blessings of creation. Help us to find the balance, O God, between giving and receiving, between doing the Word and inhabiting the Word. Help us to know when our place is in the kitchen and when it is at your feet. In Christ's name we pray. Amen.

Assurance of Grace

It is enough. Asking is enough. Stopping is enough. We sit at Christ's feet and learn the holy quiet of forgiveness.

Anna Shirey

Spring Break Prayer

To those college students on their spring break, O God, we send our love.
Accompany them during their travels.
Remind them of your presence in the midst of their celebrations.
Grant them your joy in their work and play.

To those college students on their spring break, O God, we give our support.
Move with them in their disappointments and fears.
Take them in your loving care in the midst of their failings.
Delight with them in their life-changing experiences.

We cannot always be present with college students, O God.
But we trust your presence with them.
We trust their educational experiences, at the college campus and beyond.
We thank you that they are coming into their own as beloved images of God.

Katherine Low

FOR CHRISTIAN EDUCATION SUNDAY, THE RESTARTING OF A CHURCH'S EDUCATIONAL MINISTRY PROGRAMS, OR ANY SUNDAY WHEN TEACHING AND LEARNING ARE CELEBRATED.

Psalm 78:1–7, Mark 10:13–16

A Service of Commitment to Teaching and Learning

ONE: Today we celebrate the educational ministries in our church by giving thanks for those who teach and for those who learn. When Jesus called the little children to him and placed them at the center, he showed us that a child can teach and that an adult can continue to learn. We are all teachers. We are all learners. As we grow and live through each new life experience, God remains with us, and we come to know God in new ways.

CHILD: I want to learn how to talk with God. I know God is here with me, but it's hard to know what to say to someone I can't see.

YOUTH: I am discovering who I am, but with sports and homework and friends, I'm wondering where God fits into my life. I'm not even sure that I really fit in here at church. I need someone to help me understand the things that are so hard to believe in right now.

YOUNG ADULT: I have so many questions and everyone is giving me different answers. I want to share what I'm learning about God with others who also ask questions.

ADULT: I once thought I knew everything. Now that I'm older, I can see that there is still much to learn. I wonder if these Bible stories I read as a child will speak differently to me today.

ONE: We are never too old to stop learning and we are never too young to start. Everything we do at our church is an opportunity for learning. We need to remember that a tiny infant has as much to teach us as the wisest elder.

CHILD: I can show you how to praise God on Sunday morning with your loudest and happiest singing voice. I know Jesus loves me and I can show it when I dance and when I clap my hands.

YOUTH: You may think that I'm self-centered from the way I behave sometimes, but I want to reach out and help people in need. Just give me a rake or a shovel and I'll show you God's love for others.

YOUNG ADULT: I still have questions about God's will for my life, but that's okay. I think asking questions helps us all to learn more. What questions do you have? I'll be happy to ask you mine!

ADULT: Well, I figure at this point I've seen it all, so I can share my experiences of God's presence in my life with both kids and adults who are on this journey with God, too.

ONE: Since we are all children of God, each one of us has something to teach and share with one another. God meets each of us where we are and God's love allows us to serve as Christian role models to young and old alike. Let us join in covenanting together as a teaching and learning community in Christ.

ALL: We affirm that the teaching ministry in our congregation is a gift from God as well as our own responsibility. We will tell our children what we have heard and known from our biblical ancestors—the glorious deeds and wonders God has done. We commit to passing on our faith to the next generations, and to sharing our faith with each other as we grow together in God's love. We will offer our guidance and support to the educational ministries of this church through teaching, learning, the gifts of our time and talents, and prayer. We promise all this for the sake of our Teacher, Jesus Christ. Amen.

Deborah Gline Allen

Children's Moment on Job

So school is starting . . . what does that mean? Bullies!

Why are there bullies? Why do we coop kids up in school when the weather is nice? Why aren't all teachers really nice? Why do good dogs get hit by cars but the bitey-barky dogs seem to live forever?

These are very good questions. Unfortunately I don't have very good answers. When I was a kid I hated it when people talked down to me. I hated it when I couldn't do something and I would ask, "Why?" and the only answer I got was, "Because you are a kid and too young."

"Why can't I use the chainsaw?" "You're too young!" Maybe I'm still to young because I got a lump on my shin with a chainsaw recently.

Today Job gets the answer kids too often get. *(Tell the story of Job. Broke after being rich. Kids killed. Painful disease.)* After all that God says, "Listen! I am God—you aren't! You can't figure out how I got the universe going. You will not understand why these bad things happen to you. But know I am God. I'm sorry these bad things happen to you. My son Jesus came so that the bad things would never win in the end. The New York Yankees might be up three games to nothing, but the Red Sox won four in a row and the World Series." (2004)

Brian Grover

18

OF EARTH AND SKY

Liturgy Based In Natural Imagery

AND TO THE ANGEL OF THE CHURCH
IN LAODICEA WRITE: THE WORDS OF
THE AMEN, THE FAITHFUL AND TRUE WITNESS,
THE ORIGIN OF GOD'S CREATION.

Revelation 3:14

Opening Prayer . Psalm 29:11; 147:4, 14

God of calmness, we know you're here. You see our slightest movement. You hear our every breath. Be with us and help us to feel your presence. Awaken our senses. Help us to know your warmth through the sun on our skin. Help us to feel your strength with each step we take on the firm ground. Help us to smell your sweetness in the fragrance of the flowers that fills the air. Help us to see you in the bright constellations. We know you're here. Surround us. Amen.

Kendra Purscell

God of grace and glory, creator of peaks, plateaus, buttes, and washes, you call each one of us by name for we are your children. In the velvet night under your myriad stars, speak to us through the night winds, slow and haunting. We restlessly wait for your Spirit and your Word. Wrap us in wonder and rock us gently like a mother rocks her child.

Susan Hodge-Parker

Invocation

God of the mountains and valley, oceans and streams, cities and suburbs, we open our hearts to you. Hear our prayers and hymns of praise. Fill us with hope. Gently heal our brokenness and touch our hearts with your love. Open our hearts to your presence and help us love you every day of our lives.

Frances A. Bogle

Please, God, let me never take for granted the beauties and wonders of nature. Let me never look with jaundiced eyes at a sunrise or a sunset, without feeling that they are truly religious happenings. Let me always be filled with pleasure at seeing the first crocus pushing its way up through the hard, cold ground, the new leaves appearing on the trees, the little striped chipmunks darting from place to place, the robins looking for food for the new little ones waiting to be fed. Let me always look to the sky, to see the beauty of the clouds and feel the warming rays of the sun. You have given us such a beautiful world; help me to always marvel at it and enjoy it. Amen.

Isabel Grasso

The rain smells so powerful. The earthy smell rises when it falls and the air empties itself of the grime of this world. Wash my spirit with your cleansing rain, God. Force the potential you have put in my heart to rise and burst with exciting growth. Remind me of the freshness that filled the earth after the flood. Force the flood waters from my soul to expose the freshness of being your child. Amen.

Arlene L. Drennan

Heavenly Gardener, as the sunlight is transformed into energy by plants, let your light shining upon us transform us. Let your word sown in our hearts blossom into amazing acts of love and service. Open us to your presence and fill us with your spirit so that we may reflect your love for all people. Let others experience your warmth and love through us. Amen.

Susan Hodge-Parker

Loving God, you give us the earth, the sky, the sea, this land to call home, a universe of wonders, and half a million hours or so to search its mysteries. You give us companions for the journey, and send us your Christ, the Author of truth and love, to show us the way. Accept, O God, our hearts, our praise and these gifts, which say we know from whom all blessings flow. Amen.

David Slater

Confession

Holy God, we turn to you with heavy hearts. We confess that there have been times when we have turned away from you. We have also turned away from our families and loved ones. We have hurt ourselves and hurt the earth. Forgive us, and teach us to forgive ourselves and each other. Help us believe in your love especially when we feel the most unlovable. May the joy of Jesus' resurrection fill us with renewed hope and belief in the possibility of change in our lives. In Jesus name we pray, Amen.

Frances A. Bogle

Confession

For the beauty of the earth—that we have not seen,
For the beauty of the earth—that we have not preserved,
For the beauty of the earth—that we have damaged
    or been silent at its destruction,
Forgive us, God.

For the joy of human love—that we have ignored,
For the joy of human love—dying while we watch another channel,
For the joy of human love—that we damage by our personal sins
    and faraway complicities,
Forgive us, God. Amen.

Assurance of Grace

God teaches us to raise a song of praise, not only with our lips open, but with widespread hearts and hands. We are forgiven and given responsibility again— for the beautiful earth and all aspects of human love. Amen.

Maren C. Tirabassi

Benediction

Go in peace, my friends. Celebrate the wonders of creation, and know that in all of the seasons of our lives God is with us. Listen to the songs of the waves and the hymns of the trees. Touch the earth with love and respect. May God bless us and hold us gently as we seek to do God's work in the world. Our service has ended. Our service begins. Amen.

Frances A. Bogle

19

ON OUR HEARTS
A Diversity of Prayers

AMEN! BLESSING AND GLORY AND WISDOM
AND THANKSGIVING AND HONOR
AND POWER AND MIGHT
BE TO OUR GOD FOREVER AND EVER! AMEN.

Revelation 7:12

A Prayer For New Beginnings

God, you have delivered a new beginning to me. A door that I wasn't looking for has now been opened. Keep my eyes focused on your perfect plan as I venture through this portal. Help me to use this opportunity to glorify you and grow in faith as your child. Your glory shines in beginnings. Amen.

Arlene L. Drennan

A Prayer for the Senses

Ever-speaking God, do you have a Word for us this night?
Will your whisper resound in our ears?

Speak to us, we pray.

Ever-listening God, have you inclined your ear as our voices rise?
Shall you be attentive to us as we question and converse?

Hear us, we pray.

Ever-seeing God, might you peer into our lives in this hour?
Can you spy in us a hint of growth from experiences gone by?

Watch over us, we pray.

Ever-embracing God, are you going to touch our souls this evening?
Please, trace the outline of our lives with your divine hand.

Embrace us, we pray.

Ever-appetizing God, will you spread before us a feast of blessing?
Grant us a foretaste of your Kin-dom.

May we feast of your goodness this night!

Leah Robberts-Mosser

Prayer for Children

Heavenly Parent, you nourish us all with food and with blessings. Strengthen
my children with the food that we prepare together and with the warmth of
our nearness. Help me to appreciate and nurture the unique spirits that you
have entrusted to my care so that they may grow to love and serve you. Amen.

Susan Hodge-Parker

Prayer for Surrogate Mothers

Gracious God of birth and born again, we give you thanks for surrogate
mothers who follow in the tradition of people with unfamiliar names like
Bilhah and Zilpah. May their pregnant months be blessed, may their health
be sustained, and may the surge of emotion not overflow the shoreline of
dedication. Bless the parents who receive each newborn child with joy and
wisdom, gratitude and a sense of boundaries. We pray in the name of Jesus
Christ, whose nativity helps us explore the geography of parenthood. Amen.

Prayer for Surrogate Parents

Bless all surrogate parents that they may be like Eli and Mordecai, Pharaoh's
daughter and Naomi—caregivers and guides of those who are most vulnerable. May all children with disabilities who need surrogates for health and
education concerns find a nurturing adult. Embrace, O God, those who foster and are fostered in this and more traditional ways and those who admin-
ister programs—with wisdom, perseverance and compassion. We pray in the
name of Jesus, who was educated at Joseph's knee. Amen.

Maren C. Tirabassi

I See People Like Trees · Mark 8:22–26

Once, like one born blind to Christ,
I saw people only as trees,

fixed in some forest through which I stumbled,
camouflaged by limb and leaf.

but now these many trees around,
growing fast and cutting down

I see they are people too
and marvel at their knotted wood.

William B. Jones

Grandfather's Prayer

I'm grateful for the cycles of life and the deep truth—for everything there is a season.

I am grateful for the ongoing joy of being a grandfather and the momentary joy of my daughter receiving from her grandfather—great-grandmother's rocking chair.

Yet this joy is muted because her own grandmother is moving into what may be Alzheimer's disease—a journey where the stories are lost though the cycle goes on. Thank you, God, for seasons and story, for special gifts and for the love of family in spite of everything—all intimations of your love for all of your creation. Amen.

Randall L. Hyvonen

The Steering Wheel

I giggled when this came to mind.
Then I thought about it;
It really is my daily mandala.
It is with me when I go anywhere.
The endless journeys

To dance with my daughter who wants to be on Broadway,
To play practice, to soccer, to baseball, to softball, to basketball,
To high school, to middle school, to primary school, to preschool
To church, to eldercare, to seminary, to youth group.

I hold it as my two girls and I sing Amazing Grace
And I wonder what grace exists in my life that allows me to sing this
With two teenage girls.
I clutched it the many times when I went to see my dying father.
Tears flowed upon it freely when he left this earth.
It trembled in my hands the day my ten-year-old son
told me he was so sad all the time.
I grasped it with anxious hands the first time I took my husband to chemo.

But—when I am with it by myself—I pray for my day.
For my family.
For the patients at the hospital.
For the intimate.
For the worldly.
I contemplate my path, my existence, my journey.
And I give thanks.

Yes, it is mundane. Ordinary. Silly.
But—It gets me where I need to go.
Amen.

Anne-Marie Davenport

Illuminating God, thank you for safe journeys, shared laughter, and shared sorrows. Help us to be the people that you yearn for us to be: sustained by faith; brave, loving, forgiving, and wise. Bless your broken children that they may be made whole. Bless those who mourn so that they can be comforted and healed. Bless us all. Amen.

Susan Hodge-Parker

Meditation for Troubled Times and a Shortage of Faith

Imagine being blindfolded. It's dark, silent, and you don't know what or who is around you. You try to keep your mind level, assessing the situation for possible options. Suddenly you feel a pair of hands take yours and pull you in some direction. You are unsure of what to do. If you let them move you, your location may no longer be known to you. On top of things, your guide remains anonymous. Will you let this stranger direct you? Or will you struggle and try to break away?

In today's world, most people would not trust another person with their life. They become rigid, unmovable, refusing to be steered by someone else. People always want to be in control of a situation, a machine, or another person. Perhaps it is a lack of faith in the world.

It is no surprise that, with wars and terrorists, infidelity and breakups, hate crimes and murders, liars and cheaters, there is a shortage of faith. The mind that sees violence and destruction is greatly impacted, more so than the mind that cannot see humanity's goodness. So how can you instill trust in something invisible? How can you fight doubt?

Perhaps the barrier that separates you from trusting others is in your mind and heart. You must find a way to break down that obstruction and let others in. You must also take action within society, so that people are able to see the goodness of human nature. And, most importantly, you must put your faith in God, who will never let you down. God not only shows the way but carries you through the shadowy times of your life. God gives you the ability to have faith, because you do not know if there will be a day when you need the hand of another to guide you through the darkness.

When you seem to be losing faith, say this little prayer:

Hi, God. I feel lost. So I am reaching out to you. Please take my hand and guide me through the dark. I know you will not let go. I know I will get to that unknown destination with you. My heart tells me that I will always have you there to guide me. Please help me get through whatever hardship lies in my path. Thank you.

Lauren Kay Tortal

Prayer for Farmworkers

God of the Universe, whose first home was a garden and who causes rain to fall and seeds to grow, bless our farms and all those who work the land. As you walked in the Garden of Eden by the side of Adam and Eve, softly tread the ground beside us. More than a job or profession, farmers are called to a way of life. In the dust of the earth, may we feel your breath stir us to life and faith. In the sweat of our brow, may we recall the tears of Christ on our behalf. As we sow, let some of our seed be gospel grain. As we reap, may we bring in a harvest of righteousness to our God. Amen.

Sheryl Stewart

Prayer for Clergy · Isaiah 50:4–9a; Psalm 116:1–9

O God, help us understand that, as we answer your call to serve others, there may be those who will not respond as we would hope—those who may want to humiliate us or insult us or strike out against us. Help us to remember that when we reach out to you, you will hear our cries and give us the gifts we need: You will give us tongues to teach; you will open our ears to hear; and you will give us the strength to be firm like flint . . . all so that, as we respond to others, we mirror your constant grace and mercy. Amen.

Randall L. Hyvonen

Prayer Upon Entering a Labyrinth

O God of many paths,

We stand before you at this labyrinth today as a metaphor of our journey with you. We so often behave as if the shortest distance between two points is a straight line. We are somewhat impatient, we are uncomfortable waiting, and we'd prefer to find you by way of a straight line. O God of infinite patience, you have brought us here to a different path, a curved path, a path that more closely resembles life itself. So we will put one foot in front of the other, and even though it may seem at times as if we are straying from you, we actually will be drawing closer to you all the time. So as we enter this symbol of our surrender to mystery, we promise to trust that this path, which curves in and then out again, will ultimately lead us to the Center—which is you. Amen.

Deborah Gline Allen

Prayer for Daily/Weekly Spiritual Practice

May this discipline descend me into the depths of encounter with you, O God.
May my dedication divert me from doubt.
May my devotion propel me forward with momentum.
May passion ignite my inertia and free me from boredom.
May my practice hold me steady amidst chaos within and around me.
May breath help me to sustain a healthy pace.
May my prayers grant me endurance for the long haul.
May I hurl myself over plateaus and not rest too proudly when I'm at peak performance. And, on the days when I bypass the need for practice, guide me ever so gently to sustained commitment to show up for myself, to show up for you,

no matter the excuse I've conjured. Keep teaching me. I'll keep learning. Bless my path of practice with refreshing insight and enduring wisdom. Amen.

Elizabeth D. Barnum

Prayer of Confession Based on the Three "Versions" of the Lord's Prayer
Matthew 6:9–13; Luke 11:2-4

O Holy God in heaven, through your Son, Jesus Christ,
and with the encouragement of your Holy Spirit,
you have taught us to pray for our selves and the world:

Forgive us our debts.

**We know that we have not ensured every human being
those qualities of life that you call us to provide.**

We admit the part we owe to the debts of
freedom, security, equality, and identity, for all people.

Have mercy on your people gathered here, O Lord.

Forgive us our trespasses.

**We know that we have sometimes invaded
the boundaries of other peoples' lives so that
we might have the best and most for our own lives.**

Because we have not always respected the lives of others,
the poor are still poor, the hungry are still hungry,
and the invisible are still invisible.

Have mercy on your people gathered here, O Lord.

Forgive us our sins.

**We know that we have turned our hearts away from you.
Through private thoughts or public actions,
we have rebelled against your laws and your will.
As individuals and as a community,
we confess that we have not kept your commandments.**

We have not loved you.
We have not loved others.
We have not loved ourselves.

Have mercy on your people gathered here, O Lord.

Help us to forgive.

We have not received what we expected.
Our lives have been stepped on.
We have been hurt by the disobedience of others.

Forgive us as we forgive our debtors;
as we forgive those who have trespassed against us;
as we forgive those who have sinned against you.

Have mercy on your people gathered here, O Lord.

O God, we ask for your forgiveness, even as you have already forgiven us.

In the name of Jesus Christ, we are forgiven!

We ask for the transforming power of the Holy Spirit
to guide us on our path of repentance.

For thine is the kingdom, the power, and the glory, forever. Amen.

Susan E. Brown

Prayer at Time of Crisis

O God, despite our trials and tribulations,
remind us that in your love there's no need
to be anxious. You are our rock and salvation.
Hold us in your holy bosom
when we are wronged or abused
or suffer in your name.
Continue to work through us
and in us so that we
may be better servants of yours
and those around us may see your light in us.

Barbara Smith

CONTRIBUTORS INDEX

SCRIPTURE INDEX

TOPIC INDEX